WALLACE LOCKHART is a founder member of the highly acclaimed group Quern where he plays mandolin and concertina, and admits to being a struggling song-writer, a well-behaved back row player with Dunfermline Strathspey and Reel Society and the less vocally tuneful half of the Mountain Men. In addition to writing seven books, he has written and produced ten musical presentations based on various aspects of Scottish life.

There are few better qualified to write about our native fiddle and folk scene than Wallace Lockhart. For years, Scottish music has been part of his life and as one who has lived outwith Scotland, he knows from experience the importance of Celtic music as the link which keeps the homeland to mind.

D1462080

By the same author:
Highland Balls and Village Halls, New Edition 1997 (Luath Press)
On the Trail of Robert Service, 1991 (Luath Press)
The Scots and Their Oats, Fifth Edition, 1997 (Birlinn)
The Scots and Their Fish, Fifth Edition, 1997 (Birlinn)

Fiddles and Folk

GW LOCKHART

Luath Press Limited

EDINBURGH

www.luath.co.uk

First Edition 1998

The paper used in this book is
produced from renewable forests
and is chlorine-free.

Printed and bound by
Gwasg Dinefwr Press Ltd., Llandybie

Typeset in 10.5 point Sabon by
S. Fairgrieve, Edinburgh, 0131 658 1763

Contents

Introduction

I MUST HAVE BEEN sent to music at a very early age. There is a photograph in the house that shows me, well below school age, holding a conductor's baton. There I stand surrounded by a circle of children armed with a selection of tambourines, triangles and other percussion instruments. Of this band's practice sessions I have no recollections. My only memory is of making, not for the first time, a fool of myself on stage. The percussion band took part in a musical evening in our local church (I am sure we were not the stars) and after we had performed our little jingle-jangle piece, on receiving the first applause of my life, I bowed to the audience from the podium. I then turned my back on the audience, and to the accompaniment of guffaws, gave a deep bow to the band. Whether the laughter stemmed from my actions, or the shortness of my kilt as seen from the rear, I never found out, but a number of whispered comments about the incident seemed to linger for a few days.

There is no doubt I was sent to the piano before I was ready for it and I hated it like poison. As a youngster I was cowboy mad and the one instrument I wanted to play was the guitar. The only association my piano teacher had with life on the range was a bovine expression on her face and quickness on the draw with a ruler across the fingers when it was obvious I hadn't done my homework. Victory came about the age of 12. My father found another way to waste his money and Miss X and I parted company.

The teenage years were full of singing. There were the songs at home and the songs we sang when out on our bikes or camping. At school we were nourished on polite Scottish songs (I still hate 'Kelvingrove') and pushed, willingly, to Gilbert and Sullivan (where we could adjust the words) and less willingly to more classical material. My father loved the variety theatre and I never refused an offer to accompany him. There I learned something I have never forgotten, audience snobbishness. Singers would belt out the standards 'Wee Cooper of Fife' or 'Bonnie Wells o' Wearie', to reasonable applause. Then as a special treat, they would tackle something from the classics. Nothing too classical you understand: I once heard 'Donkey Serenade' being so described. Classic evidently meant not Scots. And after this offering, the singer would leave the stage to thunderous clamourings. The rest of my musical education came from the radio. Country dance bands flourished. This was the beginning of the great era of Shand, MacLeod, Cameron, Hannah and Powrie when crowds would follow specific bands to their gigs. The conventional dance bands, more British than American, played the sweetest of music in a country full of ballrooms. Yet anomalies did exist. Boys learning the fiddle carried it a little self-consciously to music lessons. The guitar was still something attached to a cowboy's horse.

In my late teens I reached a musical landmark. I heard a piece of music which took my breath away. The tune was Duke Ellington's 'Solitude' and I knew I had to be able to play it. The music was purchased and for the first time in years I sat at the piano, looking aghast at hundreds of notes of different shapes and sizes, some of which I didn't know existed. How long I slaved over 'Solitude' I do not remember, but master it I did, and today it is still the only tune I can play from memory on the piano. It seems amazing to me now that I was able to record myself singing and playing that tune all those years ago. Studios didn't come cheap even then, and I certainly wasn't wealthy. But I do have the record to prove it. My singing on it is unbelievably bad and still guaranteed to produce hysterical laughter.

When I was in the forces I used to meet an old friend from home occasionally at a really huge club for service people in Chester. It possessed a magnificent grand piano and the sound system extended throughout the building. My old friend, who has been very good at getting me into trouble over the years, encouraged me to sit at the piano and play 'Solitude'. This I did, giving it all the flourish and expression I could muster. I finished to great cheers and cries for more. As I couldn't play anything else, I modestly indicated I didn't want to hog the piano and moved away. A few minutes later a most attractive WREN (a kind of lady sailor) approached me and asked if I would play especially for her. She was very pretty and there was a feeling of chemistry in the air. I thought hard and tried out a one-finger 'In The Mood'. Was it C-E-G or D-F-A? I didn't know, I couldn't do it. Feeling, I suppose, I was being rude to her, she turned away and walked out of my life. How I cursed not persevering with my piano lessons!

However as interest in Scottish culture dimmed around the mid-fifties, we saw all our cultural bits and pieces packed into a number of tidy boxes. Pipers played in pipe bands devoted to obtaining credit in a world of competitions. Jackets were no longer hung on hooks in village halls as country dancing became a night class item where one went to learn that 'paddy ba' was really pas de basque and that bruised arms need not be synonymous with birling. Those intent on singing joined choirs where the songs came from printed material. Short supply fiddlers joined orchestras to practise for a few concerts a year. To write in these terms is not to denigrate those who pursued our traditions as hobbies. They kept a culture alive and gave us a base on which the future could be built. And many, of course, fought long and hard to stop the decline from worsening. But in boxes we did exist.

Around this time, I had the good fortune to travel widely in North America and experience American and Canadian folk singers and musicians close up. The odd thing was their names and voices didn't linger with me the way I would absorb, say, Jim Reeves after years back in this country. Later, when living in England I developed a craze for French cafe music. This eased off when a favourite singer put on weight and her love songs didn't, to me, have the same realism. Occasional journeys north allowed me see Andy Stewart on the stage and I returned south to make my family home-sick and bore my friends with the songs that were making him famous. I don't think the permanent residents of Scotland ever realised how much Andy Stewart meant to exiles.

Around the mid-sixties, one could sense that something was happening in the music scene in Scotland. An interest was awakening in the three traditional instruments, fiddle, pipes and clarsach. Folk songs that hadn't been heard for long enough began to be heard once more. America not only produced folk singers with charisma that our young people sought to emulate, but by basing Polaris submarines in the Holy Loch allowed Scotland to have its own flourishing protest song movement. Not living in a house amenable to such protests, there was a feeling of guilt attached to playing and listening to Joan Baez, my favourite female singer of all time. Anyway, by the time I returned to Scotland the folk scene was well established and clubs and festivals were gathering a head of steam. They comfortably picked up much music from earlier years.

So we now look back over a vastly changed scene. While country dancing evening classes still exist, young people in their hordes attend ceilidh dances, happily assimilating up the steps as they go along. Pipers have crossed the divide into folk groups and we bless the day the possibilities of the small pipes were recognised. The guitar was eventually taken up as the outstanding accompaniment to a folk singer. Considering it was a stock item in Nathaniel Gow's shop two hundred years ago there is wonder about the delay. There then seemed to be the sudden discovery (known long enough in Shetland) that the guitar was a superb instrument for backing fiddles and it moved into a new function. A more enlightened education policy offered instrument playing at school and the uptake was wide and enthusiastic. Cape Breton is now a name on the lips of everyone with an interest in Scottish music. Many individuals and groups have in recent years visited Cape Breton to experience the music, the hospitality and the unbelievable Scottishness of the place. The urge to bring Scotland and Nova Scotia into closer union is stirring.

It is good to see the way the barriers between the different facets of our music have completely broken down. Eddie McGuire of the Whistlebinkies writes music for the Scottish ballet, Hamish Moore on the small pipes joins Dick Lee on clarinet in a series of swing concerts, folk fiddlers freelance with classical orchestras, the assistant conductor of the Scottish Fiddle Orchestra plays with the Ceilidh band Coila, the clarsach becomes not only a solo but a group instrument, strathspey and reel societies offer guest spots

to folk singers while the banjo may be seen in a country dance band. There is virtually no restriction on instruments. Perhaps most important of all, young people in particular are learning to play and to take an interest in the Scottish cultural scene, to regard it as our natural heritage.

Today people are singing and making music the way the mood takes them. I believe this not only stimulates creativity but coming from the heart (or grass roots if you prefer) strengthens the culture. Of course there are some who shake their heads, and of course there are

Boys of the Lough

4

dangers ahead. Increasing communication between countries means we are open to more influences. An increasingly multi-cultural society will, I believe, lead to an acceptance of things we have hitherto rejected. We are currently in a period of experimentation. I cannot say I like what some music groups are doing, especially where they associate progress with decibel levels. But evolution is always with us, we ignore it at our peril. What is good will last; what is not will fall by the wayside.

For myself, I have lost the battle with the piano, and after experimenting with the guitar and cello have found happiness with the mandolin and concertina. My involvement in writing and producing some ten musical journeys on Scottish literary figures and aspects of Scottish life has provided the impetus to delve into Scottish music to a depth I never knew existed. My playing with the Quern has provided travel opportunities to meet with performers from many countries. A little success in song-writing has come my way.

In *Fiddles and Folk*, I have tried to avoid a formal approach to Scottish music as it affects those of us with our musical heritage coursing through our veins. The picture I have sought is one made up of many brush strokes, looking at how some individuals and groups have come to the fore, examining their music, lives, thoughts, even philosophies. Everyone approached was happy to talk without restriction. They have given me an added pride in the culture of my country. I hope this book will do the same for you.

CHAPTER I

Enter the Folk Song

*There war never ane o' my sangs prentit till ye prentit
them yoursel', and ye hae spoilt them awthegither. They were
made for singin' an' no for readin'; but ye hae broken the
charm noo, and they'll never be sung mair.*

Margaret Laidlaw speaking to Sir Walter Scott

*If a man were permitted to make all the
ballads, he need not care who should make all
the laws of a nation.*

Andrew Fletcher of Saltoun (1655-1716)

AT ONE OF THOSE cosy little gatherings one lands in from time to
time, an old gentleman sang a song which started:
*When I was a young lad working at the smiddie-o
I wore a lang coat, just like my Daddie-o.*
To be truthful, it wasn't much of a song, but a young girl pre-
sent was quite entranced by it and insisted on learning the words.
It was an example of the oral tradition at work.

The above, of course, does not represent an isolated occurrence.
Along with crack and good company, Scots like to sing. The oral
tradition is strong. Most are capable of rendering a few verses that
have found their way down the family tree. Street songs and bothy
ballads, polite schoolday melodies ('Will Ye Come to Kelvingrove?'), bawdy offerings from later years, historical rousers and
attacks against society make us what we are. And while our tastes
may vary, underneath there is a feeling our songs unite us. How
many nations could think of something as folksy as 'Flower of
Scotland' being national anthem material?

Although it can be argued the distinction is becoming rather
blurred, it has long been a practice to identify our musical voice
expressions as either folk-songs or ballads. John Ord in his *Bothy
Songs of Aberdeen, Banff and Moray* could be quite precise (if a
little patronising) in his definitions:

'Folk-song means briefly that body of minstrelsy which circulates among the common people of the country, and has originated among them. It is a communal product, and not, as a rule, the result of individual effort. A ballad is a species of minor epic; that is, it narrates a story, real or fictitious, representing some heroic action or event of lasting importance in the history of a nation or race, or it may be some long forgotten love tragedy, or dark deed of revenge'.

Louis Armstrong, that magnificent trumpeter of yesteryear, saw things in simpler terms: 'All music's folk music: leastways I never heard of no horse making it.'

Ord might have added the ballad can be both real and fictitious at the same time. In view of the many arguments that have raged over 'The Queen's Maries', or 'Mary Hamilton' as it is often called in old books, let us spend a minute or two on this favourite. The four little girls chosen to attend the young princess when she was sent to France at the age of six, and who returned with her to Scotland as Ladies in Waiting in 1561 were the Maries – Seaton, Beaton, Carmichael and Livingstone. There was a French waiting-woman who was hanged for murdering the illegitimate infant she bore to the Queen's apothecary. Has she a connection with the

The High Level Ranters, a
hugely influential folk group

song? Evelyn Wells in her book *The Ballad Tree* has some interesting comments to make:

'The fact would seem to be that a series of folk-singers, picking up the gossip and rumour of Mary's court, combined into one story the authentic Maries, other ladies bearing famous Scottish names who might or might not be named Mary and about whom scandal was whispered though not recorded, and the Queen's French waiting woman (confused with lady-in-waiting), whose tragic affair with the apothecary was a matter of fact and record.

The ballad, as it has been recently recovered in Scotland and America, [Wells was writing fifty years ago] has shrunk to four or five stanzas, the 'Four Maries' lines, and the lament of a girl dying in a foreign country for a crime she hopes her parents will never know about. A Scotchwoman who sang the song to me recently knew only these verses, and gave one reason for the loss of the rest: "My parents were so cautious and discreet, they never told me the whole story".'

Adaptation and evolution and, and as we have seen from the above example, selection of part of a tale, have played a big part in our folk song scene. Rhymer A writes something, Rhymer B adds a verse and changes a couple of A's lines. Years later Rhymer C adds another verse and to be cussed, decides the words sit more comfortably with different or varied music. But normally, the tune is the vehicle. At the gathering I have referred to above, we had disagreement. When we got to 'The Auld Meal Mill' the words trotted out were:

When the horse are in the stable,
And the kye are in the byre,
And the hard day's work is over
And the auld fowk roond the fire.

But the earlier generation present declared the old words to be superior:

O my mother's flyt-in at me,
For no bidin' mair at hame,
Sayin' I'm a lazy limmer,
An' a glaiket, senseless dame.

For the greatest number of word variations on a tune, 'John Anderson, My Jo' cannot be far away from the prize list. The Burns words we hear every January are the first that come to mind:

8

John Anderson my jo, John,
When we were first acquent;
Your locks were like the raven,
Your bonie brow was brent.

Those who like to keep a copy of *The Merry Muses* on the shelf will remember Jean's pleas to her husband to come to bed:

John Anderson, my jo, John,
I wonder what ye mean,
To lie sae lang i' the mornin',
And sit sae late at e'en?

An earlier version though saw John Anderson as a man more interested in drink than home comforts:

John Anderson, my jo John,
I wonder what you mean,
Ye're goin' on the spree, John.
And stayin' oot at e'en.
This leads on to that lovely verse that starts:
Ye're going to Lucky Fill the Stoups,
Ye meet wi' Cooper Will,
Ye sit and booze like silly gowks,
And aye the other gill.

David Herd in his 1776 collection sees the tune as backing for humorous verse:

When I was a wee thing,
And just like an elf,
All the meat that e'er I gat,
I laid upon the shelf.

The rottens and the mice
They fell into a strife,
They wadnae let my meat alane
Till I gat a wife.

John Anderson is one of our oldest tunes. Over forty variants have been identified. It has turned up in lands many miles across the sea.

It is not difficult to give other examples of adaptation and evolution. In the days before copyright, it was easier to think of oneself as a bard than it is today.

We are now living in a world where what we call a folk song can be a one man effort, and, because of copyright restrictions, becoming ever more severe, the published product can not be tampered with. That we must live with and the market will sort things out; the good will survive, the rubbish will perish. But have we really exhausted the past?

That many of our old folksongs have left the scene and are seldom, if ever, sung nowadays can hardly be denied. To a large extent this is inevitable. We like to move with the times and express today's world. But of course, many of our older folk songs do express today's feelings. The huge range of Jacobite songs of two centuries ago are frequently used to express a current call for nationhood. But we are forgetting that there is a huge storehouse of folk songs tidily stored away for us to use and we are being less than true to our cause, if we neglect the heritage left to us. And this reservoir of folk music and song is one that many a nation can only regard with envy. Let us skim over some of the sources that are worthy of our attention.

While we can delve into the distant past (the ballad of Sir Patrick Spens has been dated late thirteenth century by Child) a good starting place to see how much material is waiting to be used or brought up to date is the Skene MS of around 1520. There one finds the music and titles of many old airs, one of the best known being the one finding fame a century later as 'The Flowers of the Forest'. Some would claim the first proper Scottish song book to be Thomson's *Orpheus Caledonius*. The book is undated but it is generally thought its publication took place around 1725. *Orpheus Caledonius* contains such songs as 'The Lass of Paties Mill' and 'The Bonny Earl of Murray'. Anyone who would not define these songs today as folk-songs should remember that until these songs were published they must have existed solely in the oral tradition. Even after there was a certain availability of published song books, most Scots would sing the songs and pass them on unaware they existed in book form. It's a personal opinion, but it does seem a bit extreme to adopt an attitude, prevalent in some American quarters, that 'a ballad in print is a ballad already dying'.

Alan Ramsay, the Edinburgh wig-maker turned poet, patron of the arts and general literary busybody, brought together a mixed collection of old and new songs in his *Tea-Table Miscellany*. Although the *Miscellany* was popular in its time, Ramsay's tampering with the words did little to enhance the songs. Unfortunately, he also thought it unnecessary to include music, a bad habit others would pick up, and he saw himself as a defender of morality:

'In my compositions and collections, I have kept out all smut and ribaldry, that the modest voice and ear of the fair singer might meet with no affront; the chief bent of all my studies being to gain their good graces; and it shall always be my care to ward off those frowns that would prove mortal to my muse.'

Oswald's *Caledonian Pocket Companion* published in the mid-eighteenth century and which contains hundreds of fiddle tunes has become a priceless source book. This is the collection Burns drew on to provide the settings for so many of his songs. As is well known, Burns devoted his last years to somewhat altruistically seeking to preserve the speech and song of his home heath. Some of the lyrics he provided were completely his own work, others he reconstructed or improved, and in some cases he was content to marry words already in existence with appropriate tunes. And there was, as he tells us, a certain casualness about his method of composing:

'Until I am complete master of a tune in my own singing, such as it is, I can never compose for it. My way is this. I consider the poetic sentiment correspondent to my idea of the musical expression, – then choose my theme, – compose one stanza. When that is composed, which is generally the most difficult part of the business, I walk out,- sit down now and then, – look out for objects in Nature round me that are in unison or harmony with the cogitations of my fancy, and workings of my bosom, humming every now and then the air, with the verses I have framed. When I feel my muse beginning to jade, I retire to the solitary fireside of my study, and there commit my effusions to paper, swinging at intervals on the hind legs of my elbow-chair, by way of calling forth my own critical strictures, as my pen goes. Seriously, this, at home, is almost invariably my way. What cursed egotism.'

Burns was at the time working with others on the *Scots Musical Museum* and would be dead before it was published. Around a quarter of the 600 songs in the six volumes originated from him, either directly from his own pen or from matching lyrics from another source to a stipulated piece of music. Today, the *Scots Musical Museum* is a major source of Scottish national song.

Important as the songs of Burns are to us, we cannot exist on a diet of Burns. David Herd's great collection of *Scottish Songs and Heroic Ballads*, first published in 1776 and subsequently up-dated, showed the extent of singing material in common use. Of particular interest is the obvious popularity of humorous songs. The 'Muckin' o' Geordie's Byre' and 'Old King Coul' make unex-pected appearances while songs of trades and of the country are prolific.

Sir Walter Scott made use of Herd's collection although his 'Bonnie Dundee' moves to a different world. Scott's martial song about the colourful soldier started life in humbler circumstances:

O have I burnt, or have I slain?
Or have I done aught injury?
I've gotten a bonnie young lassie wi' bairn,
The baillie's daughter of bonny Dundee.
... Open your ports, and let me gang free,
I maun stay nae langer in bonny Dundee.

Whatever blessings Scott had in the way of wealth and posi-tion, he knew his fellow Borderers, how to enjoy their company and where to look for the material he wished to record. His nights with companions like Hogg - 'the Ettrick Shepherd' – at Tibbie Shiel's Inn by the waters of St. Mary's Loch filled his retentive mind with songs that would see the light of day in his *Minstrelsy of the Scottish Border*. And his remarks, like his comments on Edie Ochiltree, showed how wide-ranging were his sources:

'... has been soldier, ballad-singer, travelling tinker, and is now a beggar ... An old Scotch mendicant who was news-carrier, min-strel, and sometimes historian of the neighbourhood. That rascal knows more old ballads and traditions than any other man in this and the next four parishes.'

It is the American, Francis James Child, that we have come to acknowledge as our greatest ballad scholar. And Child knew what it was to struggle with Scottish indifference. After sending out an inquiry for ballads to a list of Scottish schoolmasters he would lament to a colleague:

'A very large and wearisome part of my preparation has been the endeavour to stir up Scotsmen to an interest sufficient to induce them to exert themselves to save the things that may still be left. It is in vain. The Scot loves his ballads but is incurious about them.'

Child became Professor of English at Harvard University. While drawing heavily on Scott his researches indicated Scott had not been adverse to a spot of tampering with earlier material. In other words the comments of Hogg's mother Margaret Laidlaw to Scott were not without truth. Child's 25 years' study of ballads resulted in the volumes of English and Scottish Popular Ballads printed between 1882 and 1898. Child numbered the ballads in his collection from 1 to 305. Such is the authority given to him that a number quoted in brackets after the title of a ballad is sufficient to identify its source without the name Child being mentioned. Child, of course, did not supply a full complement of music to match all his ballads. It has been left to another American professor, Bertrand Bronson of the University of California to work to this end.

For a last look at collectors of yesteryear we turn to the north-east and the works of Greig and Duncan. Fortunately for us this mammoth collection has been re-edited in recent years and it is to be hoped it will not be ignored by folk-singers outwith the north-east. But two recently discovered articles by Gavin Greig prompt some thought. The first article is concerned with songs of the sea.

'Sea-songs we have in plenty, and of these the rustic singer is particularly fond; but it is quite clear that this kind of minstrelsy must have been imported. There is, however, one kind of song with which our north-east angle can claim a direct and intimate connection - the whaling song. During the earlier part of last century, when whale fishing was a great Scottish industry, Peterhead shared hon-ours with Dundee as a leading point of departure for the ships that sailed to northern waters "for to pursue the whale". The whaler's life was full of adventure; but when a crew returned "full ship" they seem to have indemnified themselves for perils past and long ban-ishment from social life by wassails that "made the taverns roar".'

So where are these sea-songs in plenty? Yes, the whaling songs are still there, 'Balena', 'Tarwathie' and the rest of them. How many songs of shellfish can you think of after Aly Windwick's 'Partans in his Creel' and Gray's 'Caller Ou'? Any songs about haddock, whit-ing or flat fish? Ewan McColl, raised in Salford, abundantly kept the herring and the fish-gutters to mind but his songs would barely qualify as shanties, not being accompaniments to work. A heritage seems to have retreated with the tide.

Greig's second article is concerned with Burns and the folk-song, and is couched in unusually strong terms:

'The songs of Burns have never been sung by our peasantry in general; or, putting it more widely, we may say that Scottish book-songs have never been the songs of the mass of the Scottish people.

This statement, as far as we know, is here made for the first time in good black print. It is to me quite astounding that the Scottish people themselves should put forward the songs of Burns, Lady Nairn, Tannahill, Hogg and Scott, as their own authentic native minstrelsy.'

And this very positive man continues:

'If any of our poet's songs is thoroughly well known it should be 'Auld Lang Syne'; and yet in a company of several hundred Scotsmen joining in its strains there may not be a single soul who knows the verses right.'

The voice of a man who collected thousands of songs in the north-east cannot be ignored. Certainly, one of the best known songs in Scotland today for community singing is 'The Northern Lights of old Aberdeen' and this song is a far remove from Burns. As one ponders Greig's statement, one sees a lot of truth in it, yet, paradoxically, we remember that many who style themselves folk-singers never fail to include something of Burns when they take the stage.

The music world has changed since Greig's day. Folk clubs, folk festivals, folk singer concert appearances, have, while creating greater interest in folk song, made the folk scene more performer focussed. I believe that those who seek to entertain from a stage, will, if not writing their own material, seek to explore the past collections, of which I have only commented on a few, much more. There is too much interest in source material, too much interest in the resurrection of old melodies for this not to happen. One of the recent delights of the folk scene has been the successful setting to music of poems that stir emotions in the breast. Jim Reid's and Jean Redpath's renderings of Violet Jacob's 'The Wild Geese' and 'Hallowe'en' respectively, more than make the point. One sees the same thing happening in North America with the verse of Robert Service.

If we are to bear in mind the songs people know and carry with them, then we cannot glide over the Scottish music hall contribution. This inevitably takes us into the world of Harry Lauder, a journey which will make some squirm. Emotional, irrational, kitsch, the adjectives are not hard to find. 'Braw bricht moonlicht nichts' where a 'deoch and doris' can be enjoyed while 'roamin' in the gloamin'. Yet, these songs were sung and enjoyed and their fellows, 'The Laddies who Fought and Won' and 'Keep Right on to the End of the Road' brought an inner strength to many. Lauder was not knighted for nothing. I read recently that these songs are not sung nowadays. Not so, ask anyone who entertains in Old Folks' Homes. These songs our old folk can still trot out along with songs from the first world war, never mind the second one. Obviously these old music hall stars, Will Fyfe and Dave Willis for example, had a charisma that made audiences want to remember their songs. The sadness today, centres on those who wearing stockings and kilt in such proximity that they are devoid of kneecaps, see themselves as protectors of our culture. But enough of such talk.

The contribution the Services have made to the folk scene is often neglected. True, respectable songs like 'Banks of Sicily' get an occasional airing, but my initial thoughts are on the many songs that were given their own words. 'Bless 'em All', for example, moved fairly quickly (at least in my regiment) from being about a troop ship leaving Bombay to a description of a pair of army trousers. No doubt the presence of favourite swear words kept these songs away from a world where they were considered unfit for the ears of ladies, but barrack-room troubadors flourished and these barrack-room ballads, to use Kipling's words, were transported across continents at an amazing speed. And, one reflects, how quickly such colourful songs get passed on through rugby and similar clubs today.

Any thoughts about holding on to the songs handed down to us

Planxty
Johnny Moynihan – Andy Irvine – Paul Brady – Liam O'Flynn – Christy Moore

15

must include mention of the work done by the School of Scottish Studies in Edinburgh and this is referred to further on. But let us get our bearings first. Not so long ago, street songs and country songs were simply part of the general social scene; a rendering of 'Nicky Tams' or 'An Auld Maid in a Garret' an acceptable party piece. But the authentic scene of these songs changed as what we now regard as old industries departed leaving a void in the landscape as well as in the Scots way of life. Shipbuilding on the Clyde crashed, the Dundee jute mills closed down, great engineering works slashed their workforces and on farms Clydesdales were replaced by tractors. Stooks and stacks gave way to the combine. The miners' row and farm servants' bothies and cottages felt the ravages of the elements as they stood empty. The sound of melodeon and ballad was silenced. Yet, in the midst of this, renewed and somewhat contradictory interest in Scottish ballad and folk-song came into being. Andy Stewart, a stage entertainer rather than singer, had extraordinary international success with re-vamped songs (he had the top three songs in the Australian charts at one time) that carried humorous and nostalgic references to Scotland. But it was not the songs owing their inspiration to misty islands and Scottish soldiers that would eventually carry the day at home. Political and protest singers were to have a field day.

There are many who accept the folk song revival started in America, attributing much to Woody Guthrie, Joe Hill and so on. A recollection is that the songs from across the Atlantic were welcomed, not because, in my own part of the country at least, we had given up things Scottish (the country dance bands were an important input to our lives), but because as a result of the cinema we were enthusiastic about American life. The songs from the States were easy to listen to and they expanded our repertoires. I travelled across the States in the fifties when a coffee and apple pie meal was not complete without the little chromium speaker at the table easing out 'On Top of Old Smokey'. Jeannie Robertson's quote about Aberdeen Folk Club, 'You don't get in there unless you are wearing a cowboy hat and spurs', speaks volumes.

Radio deserves a pat on the back for its help in promoting folk music in Scotland with a number of programmes in the fifties and sixties that showed folk music could draw on industry as well as on the rural scene for its material. And into our living rooms came Ewan MacColl whose singing of songs, both new and unearthed, let us know that one of those rare characters with ability and charisma was in the lead of a movement that was bearing on our culture. There were of course many milestones on the folk song revival road. The first People's Festival Ceilidh in August 1951 put the country's cultural wares on show and, most importantly, encouraged others to see the Edinburgh Festival Fringe as a place for Scottish music and song. Robin Hall and Jimmie Macgregor (before the latter achieved a reputation as a hill-walker and something of a media celebrity) found a regular spot on television for their music and also showed folk music had large concert appeal. Folk clubs sprang into being, and although there are thousands of people who naturally sing folk songs without ever seeing the inside of such a place, such clubs provide good nursery experience for aspiring writers, singers and musicians, as well as an opportunity for established figures to show their talents.

But not all the impetus came from the world of the folk club. Any look at the folk scene from the early sixties on, no matter how peripheral, must include comment on The Corries. For thirty years they stood, in the eyes of many, as a group apart. They brought professionalism to Scottish song. Immaculate in appearance, with real musicianship and sensitive arrangements, they filled the country's largest theatres. The protest song was not their *raison d'etre*. Songs

The Corries

from 'Peggy Gordon' to 'Ye Jacobites' were their interest. And because of their presentation, they were good television. Through their regular journeys into homes a receptive country became more aware of its culture. The singing of 'Flower of Scotland' at Murrayfield and other places is living proof of their legend.

At the very earthy level, one acknowledges with grateful thanks, the work of the School of Scottish Studies at Edinburgh University. Their field work, their identifying of material from sources so long disregarded, their recording and saving for posterity an amount of material that few would believe existed, warrants a country's thanks. Now that it has been unearthed, the storytelling, the songs, the impassioned singing of the Travelling Folk has added much to our appreciation of what we have and what we are. Who would have thought 60 years ago a Traveller would be asked to lecture in America?

In the following pages the folk song scene is pursued through the lives and eyes of a few who have made and added to its history. Some good tales lie ahead.

CHAPTER 2

Hamish Henderson

Thus ev'ry kind their pleasure find,
The savage and the tender;
Some social join, and leagues combine;
Some solitary wander.

'*Now westlin winds*' **Robert Burns** (1759-1784)

'*Folk songs bind the nation, bind all nations and all*
people with one spirit, one happiness, one paradise.

Leos Janacek (1854-1928)

LET IT BE SAID RIGHT AWAY, no short overview of Hamish Hender-son's activities can ever do justice to the man. His story is too dimen-sional, his talents too widespread. Poet, author, song-writer, folk-lorist, raconteur, translator, letter-writer, historian and much more, he is a unique character in the Scottish scene. His contribution to our culture is enormous.

Hamish Henderson's roots are in Blairgowrie, a small town in the heart of Scotland's soft-fruit growing area. Marking the edge of the Howe of Strathmore, the town's street signs are in Gaelic as well as English, suggesting An Commun Gaidhealach considered it a Highland enough place in which to hold the Mod. It is an area rich in country dance bands and country ways. Song was an early companion and he grew up with the knowledge that many of the songs sung at home and around 'Blair' were songs of the people, songs that were not found in books. His mother, he recalls, had a beautiful voice, with a special love of the old ballads.

One cannot speak to Hamish Henderson for more than a few minutes without becoming aware of his love of language. It is no surprise that he contributed poems to his primary school maga-zine, that Latin and modern languages were his later curricula favourites. With the vagueness of youth, he saw himself in the future as a writer of sorts. A family change of residence took him from Blairgowrie to Devon where an interest in local folklore manifested itself. In the middle 1930s, he went on to Dulwich

College in London. But, he is keen to emphasise, he never at any time lost contact with Scotland. It is interesting that at this English public school Hamish Henderson could study MacDiarmid at a time when he was pretty well unknown to Scottish pupils. And it was one of the Dulwich teachers who guided him to the three thousand-odd song Greig and Duncan collection at Aberdeen University where, he learned from the librarian, the collection was in no great demand.

The late 'thirties saw Hamish win a scholarship to Cambridge to study modern languages, and here we come across the first of his major escapades. After speaking very vigorously against the Nazi movement in the Cambridge Union one night, he was approached by representatives of an organisation who, after congratulating him on his debating skills, asked if he would be willing to do some work for them in Germany; work which involved making and maintaining contact with opponents of the regime. He accepted the offered assignment, had the interesting experience of being interviewed by a German Police department and arrived back in this country shortly before war was declared.

Hamish served for most of the war as an Intelligence Officer with the Highland Division in the Middle East and Italy, where, inci-

Hamish Henderson with story teller and ballad singer Duncan Williamson
in the kitchen of the Peat Inn, near Cupar

dentally, he retained for some time links with his partisan group. War could not still his love of poetry and in the desert he started work on his *Elegies for the Dead in Cyrenaica*. The bawdier verse he came across went down in his notebook. Some time after landing in Sicily he was driving round the small town of Linguaglossa when the sound of pipes drew him to a piazza. There, to cries of 'Viva la Scozia', were playing the Pipes and Drums of the Highland Division's 153 Brigade (one batallion Black Watch and two batallions of the Gordon Highlanders). The dramatic background to the scene was the volcano of Etna, smoke curling gently from its crater. As he listened, the pipes broke into 'Farewell to the Creeks' the well-known north country tune composed by Pipe Major James Robertson of Banff. 'Without hindrance' he says, 'the words came flowing to me'. And so was born that fine song, 'The Highland Division's Farewell to Sicily', sung by thousands, recorded later by Robin Hall and Jimmy Macgregor and still a firm favourite today of Anne Lorne Gillies who also recorded it.

The pipie is dozie, the pipie is fey -
He winna come roon for his vino the day.
The sky ow'r Messina is unco an' grey,
And a' the bricht chaulmers are eerie.

Sicily gave him his love of the Italian language, not to mention the poet, Dante, whose works he recites in a voice that booms.

The war over, Hamish returned to Cambridge to complete his studies. In 1946 he accepted the offer of a rent-free room in the Lochboisdale Hotel on South Uist where the owner, Finlay McKenzie, was especially keen he should finish off his war verse, although it would be the Autumn of 1948 before his Elegies for the Dead would be published. They received the Somerset Maugham Award in 1949. Although he was not done with poetry, he was never again to reach the heights he attained in his Elegies. Like Burns, he was to be drawn to the world of song. To use his own words in a later letter to Hugh McDiarmid, '... in any case I have come to set greater store by my songs "in the idiom of the people" than by other kinds of poetry that I have tried to write.' We shall return to his relationship with Hugh McDiarmid.

While on South Uist he had met the Laird of Canna, the distinguished folksong collector John Lorne Campbell. Accepting the Laird's invitation to visit Canna, he there came in contact with Seamus Ennis the Irish piper and Calum MacLean (brother of the

Hamish Henderson in his room at the School of Scottish Studies

poet Sorley) who were working on Canna in the employ of the Irish Folklore Commission. Their work fascinated Hamish who, both by instinct and army training, was a compulsive collector of yarns, poems and songs. (His Ballads of World War Two published in 1947 showed how active he was with a notebook.) Now he was to involve himself with the American collector Alan Lomax described at that time by Ewan MacColl as the most important name in American folksong circles. Lomax at the time had a commission from Columbia Records to prepare a series on folk and primitive music of the world. It is worth remembering too, that at this time that wonderful piece of equipment the portable tape recorder had arrived on the scene, a boon for collectors who could for the first time easily record words and music together in the field. A letter written by Alan Lomax to Hamish Henderson on the 20th September 1951 is worth quoting:

'I've been travelling the roads of the world, hitting the high places and the low places, the rough and the smooth, for about twenty years, recording folk songs aand ballads from all sorts of people, but I have never had such kind and warm-hearted treatment from anywhere as from the people of Scotland... What you have done, however, is to help the folksongs of your country to be better known. Thank you for your songs, which will be listened to by scholars and just ordinary people with the greatest interest and plea-sure.'

Hamish's work with Alan Lomax paid off. After a spell lectur-ing on poetry and politics at adult education courses in and around Fort William, he started his long association with the School of Scottish Studies, a Department of the University of Edinburgh. His early explorations in the field, particularly in the north-east, were to pay off handsomely. If one can talk about discovering people, he dis-covered those with a wealth of song material that was both live and alive, people whose existence he had known about, but never found. In particular, he entered the world of Jeannie Robertson and the Travelling Folk. As Alec Finlay in *The Armstrong Nose* would so succinctly put it, 'It was this cultural apartheid (the gulf between academicism and the living tradition) that he set about to remove once and for all.' His mind was occupied with thoughts of how to bring the songs and singing styles he was now encountering more into a mainstream situation.

When one attempts to talk about a movement, in this case the

Folk Revival, events do not sit tidily in chronological order. In the late nineteen forties, for instance, preparations were under way to launch Edinburgh's International Festival of the Arts. With a realisation that such a festival could and indeed most likely would ignore Scotland's indigenous culture, an Edinburgh Labour Festival Committee was formed and this Committee brought into being in 1951 the first 'People's Festival'. And while this festival brought together playwrights, poets and artists, its greatest and longest-living impact was the ceilidh which attracted singers from the Highlands, Islands and Lowlands. Such was the momentum built up by this ceilidh and the two that followed in consecutive years, that the singing of folk songs was given a new lease of life, making the soil more fertile for the likes of schoolteacher Norman Buchan who implanted interest and love of folk music into his school children. This, then, was the groundwork which would lead in due course to the folk revival. To quote Buchan:

'As I went into the Oddfellows Hall the bloody place was packed, feet were going, and it was Jimmy MacBeath singing "The Gallant Forty-Twa". Hamish had assembled these people. I'd never heard anything like this. John Strachan was singing forty verses of a ballad; John McDonald, the mole catcher, singing one or two of his own songs and bothy ballads. An amazing night for people who had never heard them before! It swept me completely off my feet.'

The 1951 Ceilidh had been such a remarkable success that there was no way it was not going to be repeated. And as 1952 was going to see Hugh MacDiarmid reach the age of 60, it was agreed that the ceilidh now being planned should be held in his honour. This, then, is a suitable place to look at the relationship between Hamish Henderson and Hugh MacDiarmid.

Since he was a boy at Dulwich College Hamish had stood in awe of MacDiarmid's talents as a poet. He frequently used the word *genius* when referring to him. One of the two books of poetry he went off to war with was MacDiarmid's *A Drunk Man Looks at the Thistle*. He had no doubt he was Scotland's second greatest poet. He went most of the way with MacDiarmid as he slew the Scottish dragons of sickly sentimentality and self-centred provincialism. He determined to make contact with him, did so, and gave him support of many kinds over the years. Their early letters published in *The Armstrong Nose* show both intimacy and complete frankness. They did of course share political leanings.

The 1952 Ceilidh was a tremendous success and it is worthwhile quoting Hamish Henderson on it:

'The veteran Barra singer Calum Johnston again sang and played the pipes; Kitty MacLeod and her sister Marietta enthralled the audience with "Cairistiona" and "Agus Ho Mhorag"; an excellent bothy ballad singer from the North-East Frank Steele, sang "Come All Ye Lonely Lovers"; the young Arthur Argo, great grandson of Gavin Greig, sang "The Soutar's Feast" in a boyish treble, and Jimmy McBeath gave of his best with "Come all ye Tramps and Hawkers".'

MacDiarmid was obviously moved by the occasion and was unstinting in his praise. Speaking in Edinburgh a year later about the event, he lauded it over the happenings of the official festival, castigated the press for ignoring it and finished up with this tribute to those who had taken part: 'It was one of the finest concerts I ever attended. These Scottish folk singers were real artistes. Everyone of them was culturally worth all the famous artistes, conductors, actors and actresses of the official festival a thousand times over.'

Even accepting that MacDiarmid's praise was a bit over the top, it does not explain his later reversal when he started to pass derogatory remarks about both folk songs and folksingers. Readers of *The Scotsman* would now feast royally as two of Scotland's intellectual finest traded argument through the paper's columns. 'The BBC gives too much time to corn-kisters,' voiced MacDiarmid (also making the point artistes would do well to extend their repertoires). 'Why', thundered Henderson, 'should singers like Jeannie Robertson be invited to perform in both America and Russia, but be so deprived of radio time in Scotland?' This 'Folksong Flyting' had one useful side effect. At a time when interest in all things Scottish was being aroused, it drew others into the fold, and particularly it encouraged the up and coming generation to explore their heritage. It added pressure to the folk song boiler.

By the time the sixties were maturing, Hamish Henderson had revealed the music and songs of the Travelling Folk to a surprised population. Writing in the late nineties, it is not easy to explain how he managed this, for certainly in those days, contact with Travelling Folk was, to say the least, at a minimum. To make the breakthrough that he did, to gain their trust to such a degree, speaks volumes about him as a person.

Hamish Henderson's work in collecting and recording for the

School of Scottish Studies was now becoming known nationally. Bearing in mind how few resources he had at his disposal compared with similar institutions in Eastern European Countries which were determined to keep track of their past, his achievements were remarkable. And on one point he was adamant. His 'discoveries' were not to be filed away in archives to gather dust. They were to be made available, to be shared with those who were in a position to develop them further. This was not necessarily a popular University view. And perhaps there was a growing appreciation too at this time that the basic culture of a country, so often expressed through its folk songs, does not conflict with its 'classical' culture. The former is frequently the starting point for something new. Evolution is always with us and one cannot look back over the past 30 years without recognising quite amazing transformations. To say that is not to argue that everything new that has flourished is acceptable to everyone. But who can deny that more people are getting enjoyment from the music and songs of Scotland than ever before.

As a collector, a recorder, and a saviour of much of what has gone before and might have been lost to posterity, Hamish Henderson's reputation is secure. His broadcasts over the years, both on radio and television, have prompted many to take a greater interest in the heritage handed down to us.

Most people who have knocked around a bit have a fund of stories and Hamish is no exception. He is a real raconteur. A favourite yarn concerns a certain Traveller who had helped him in his researches. A request came to Hamish Henderson from the BBC in London for an authentic voice for a forthcoming folk programme. The name Hamish submitted was accepted, and in due course the Traveller arrived in London to be put up, for the first time in his life, in a splendid luxury hotel, prior to the next day's broadcast. Unfortunately, and rather unkindly, the BBC left him that evening to his own resources. What does a Travelling man do on his own in London with not a friendly face in sight? In this case the Traveller's answer was to lift his melodeon and make for the street to do a spot of busking, something which at that time did not find favour with the London police. One wonders how he explained to the police that he was living in an expensive hotel. The poor man was lifted and spent the night in the cells, a far remove from the anticipated silk sheets.

Hamish Henderson of course never needs an excuse to break into song. Sometimes he seems to sing as much as he talks. But he puts a particular value on the use of songs to achieve things. He remembers how as a sergeant in the army he would make up humorous or bawdy lines for his men to sing to keep up morale when things weren't going too well. The same approach came naturally to him in the numerous campaigns he was involved in, be they anti-war or anti-apartheid, the popular and the unpopular. Some of the words of his songs of course, rose above the ordinary level. 'Free Mandela' was much used in this country and abroad. The fact he drew on a Spanish Civil War tune, 'The Army of the Ebro', (sometimes called, 'Long Live the 15th Brigade') gives an indication as to the spread of his knowledge of music. On the night Mandela was released he commented he would never have to sing the song again. Perversely, it is frequently requested of him. Perhaps the lyrics he will become most remembered for will be in his song, 'Freedom Come All Ye', the tune of which dates to the first world war pipe tune, 'The Bloody Fields of Flanders'. And it completes the circle when we recall that tune grew from the song which describes scenes from the hills, a few miles away from where Hamish was brought up:

Dae ye see yon high hills a' covered wi' snaw,
They hae pairted mony a true love but soon they'll part us
*   twa,*
Busk busk bonnie lassie, an' come awa' wi' me,
An I'll tak ye tae Glen Isla, near Bonnie Glenshee.

There is much inspiration in the works of Hamish Henderson; a prime example being the line from his first Elegy turned by Brian McNeill into his powerful song, 'No Gods and Precious Few Heroes'.

CHAPTER 3

Brian McNeill
and the Battlefield Band

*Legend can focus fact; music is often the best
lens to carry the light between the two.*
– **Brian McNeill**

THERE IS AN AURA OF POWER, almost a touch of the majestic,
about a Brian McNeill performance. True, he is a big fellow who
occupies a lot of stage, but his authority as he handles one instrument after another is complete. His material, positive, distinctive
and invariably interesting, is proferred without nonsense. One sees
a professional at work. And the word work is a deliberate choice.

Brian McNeill was born and bred in Falkirk. The town is not
only in the centre of Scotland but has been in the centre of much
history. Wallace and Charles Edward Stuart strode its paths. It is
associated with its past cattle markets, the great Falkirk Trysts
when 50,000 black cattle and a similar number of sheep would be
driven every year from the Highlands and Islands to meet up with
buyers from as far away as London. As we shall see, the past
would have an influence on the young McNeill learning the fiddle
at school.

Brian's early association with the fiddle passed through a number of enthusiasms. He wanted to be good at it, enjoyed playing in
the County Youth Orchestra, but never felt close to the instrument. Rock had arrived on the scene and a more glamorous instrument, the electric guitar, was now in his hands. He joined a rock
band, and, as he says, spent his teenage years carting amplifiers in
and out of church halls and pretending to be a rock star.

After school, the University of Strathclyde beckoned. There he
studied, unsurprisingly, English and, surprisingly, psychology. At
that time, teaching seemed a possible career. It is funny how simple events shape our future paths. One night he entered a favourite
Falkirk howff, the Wheatsheaf, to find an old gentleman in a corner playing Scots tunes on a mouth organ. A fiddle, apparently

without an owner, was lying nearby. He picked it up and was able to play along with the old lad. The combined playing excited him and encouraged a return to the instrument he had neglected. A search for suitable music followed. The finding that bore the most fruit was Dave Swarbrick's LP *Rags, Reels and Airs*. This he devoured and it provided the beginning to an appreciation of the kind of music he ultimately wanted to play.

Within a year of starting university in 1968, Brian McNeill had formed the Battlefield Band. Its name had no historical connection. It was taken from Battlefield Avenue on Glasgow's South Side where he was now living. The members, coming from different musical backgrounds, combined to play all kinds of music: rock followed jigs, reels preceded Bob Dylan and Leonard Cohen. The band played in any pub or indeed any establishment willing to give them space. It was essentially a fiddle and guitar outfit with different people drifting in and out, one short term member being a relative of the legendary and affectionately remembered box player, Will Starr. Morale jumped a couple of notches when folk clubs were discovered. Until then the group had not appreciated there might be places where an audience would sit quietly listening to them. These apprenticeship years were important ones to Brian. He was picking up and learning to play other instruments like the mandolin and concertina.

Brian McNeill

Then, as their student years ended, the group took the plunge, drifted south to play at the Newcastleton festival and crossed the Border to taste the English scene. It was a worthwhile journey. The band's horizons were stretched and the possibility of using instruments now creeping on to the scene like the bouzouki, mandocello and cittern was brought home to him. These he learned to play and of course they would become central to the distinctive Battlefield Band sound.

Un-usually for a folk group, a pedal organ had been acquired and the band made the discovery that the organ in conjunction with a cittern gave bagpipe tunes a noise, a lilt, a rhythm that while new was in keeping with the contemporary music mood. It was a prime example of McNeill experimentation although he gives credit to the fact that the group members had not been brought up to conform to any particular school of music. The experiment was to pay off handsomely.

Brittany of course being one of the many Celtic lands, hosts an abundance of Celtic festivals and events every year. In 1975, the Battlefield Band was invited to play at the Lorient Festival. Coming off stage after a well received performance, Brian was approached by the manager of a French recording company with the invitation to make a record. And so it came about that the Battlefield Band's first recording was made in Brittany, for sale primarily in France.

Things happened very quickly after this. The Battlefield Band was now making a name for itself. They were occasionally being used as the supporting band to the Boys of the Lough and this led to further recordings under the Topic label. In fact, three records were to come out within a 13-month period. Brian had now given up his job as a teacher and the band was heavily engaged on the French and German circuits. New members, Glaswegians of Irish descent, joined the band, and this brought a widening of the repertoire to include Irish music.

Brian was now starting to write his own music and songs. His first tune was called 'Modest Miss France'. In 1977 he had brought out his first solo album called 'Monksgate', where fairly traditional material was expressed with both traditional and not-so-traditional instruments. His flair being recognised, he began arranging, adapting, and writing tunes for words given to him, marrying Scottish songs to Breton tunes. When the group was preparing for their record *Home Is Where The Van Is* (Temple 1980) they needed another track, and to meet this need Brian wrote the words and music of 'Lads O' The Fair', unquestionably one of his finest compositions. He introduced it quietly to the group without mentioning it was his own work, and as from now on the compositions would flow, this is an appropriate place to look at Brian McNeill's place as songwriter.

First, his material, essentially Scottish, is not the Scotland of heathery slopes and misty glens. Faces come before places. His heroes are real. Protests are cunningly directed towards the Scots themselves. For someone who claims never to have been pressurised to learn Scottish history, his feelings for and knowledge of the past run deep. But it is the things that touch him he must write about: the contribution emigrants might have made had they stayed at home, the magnificence of Montrose. The pretences of authority irk him. He drives his points home hard. McNeill's songs are articulated like a poet. If you doubt that, try reading the words of 'The Back O' the North Wind', notice the absence of unnecessary words in his songs. Finally, sense the craftmanship contained within his music. In two of his greatest songs, 'Montrose' and 'Lads O' The Fair', he nicely leads us up the path to explosive choruses. In 'Strong Women Rule Us All' and 'No Gods and Precious Few Heroes' (which he wrote in conjunction with Hamish Henderson) the treatment is different. These are songs designed to make one think. The music works with the words to stir the listener. The intellectual content of entertainment is acknowledged.

Brian McNeill's ability with words came to the notice of a wider public with the publication in 1989 of his first novel, *The Busker*. Wisely he chose situations where his background could add authenticity. The action stretches from Spain to East Germany, allowing the author to integrate places he knows and languages he is familiar with into a story heavy on the thrills of the chase. But our hero does return to Scotland for a spell and we get a little gem of description that tells us something about the author:

'There's a smell to a good pub in Scotland, a smell that can overcome all the sourness, the squalor that lives with the drink - thick, yeasty and warm as the beer itself, overlaid with the sharp tang of the last drops of the dram wrung lovingly into the pint.'

We now await the arrival of his second novel, *To Answer The Peacock*.

Although he still rejoins them for the odd concert, in 1990 Brian McNeill left the Battlefield Band in order to devote more time to writing and other projects. With the Battlefield Band he had literally seen the world, travelling from Australia and New Zealand to Hong Kong, the States and Canada and most points between, losing track of the number of concerts given in Europe. With the Band he had given a new direction to traditional music. The sales of more than a dozen albums have confirmed the public's liking for what the Band has done.

Ever the experimenter, Brian has produced and performs an audio visual presentation which looks at emigration through the eyes of six Scots. It hardly needs to be said he has written the music and songs that carry it along. The characters that contribute to the story are Alexander Stewart, (servant to Charles Edward Stuart), Flora MacDonald, Andrew Carnegie, John Muir, Ewan Gillies from St. Kilda and his own great uncle James McNeill. This entertaining combination of music and learning is due to be followed by one devoted to examining the Scots contribution to Europe. As a solo artist he is still in demand throughout the world. He shares his solo appearances with others in various duos and groups. In the early nineties he was part of the experimental supergroup, Clan Alba, and remains committed to new paths in folk music.

About the changes in the folk scene he is fairly sanguine. As one who has thrived on experimentation he welcomes it in others. The public, he reckons, will decide what innovations will last. One suspects he thinks it is not only folk music that is worth experimenting with. There is a small mountain of Scottish music lying ignored because it bears a classical tag.

CHAPTER 4

Eddie McGuire
and
the Whistlebinkies

On harp or flute full merrily they playit,
And sang ballettis with michty notis clear.

"The Golden Targe" – **William Dunbar (1460?-1520?)**

GLASGOW HAS ALWAYS BEEN AN unusually musical city. The craze
for the new, country and western or rock and roll, has always sat
comfortably with the old, be it the music brought to the city by the
Gael or by the choirs and orchestras woven into the fabric of the
place. It was never a surprise the accolade of City of Culture
should reach Glasgow in 1990. The interest in all kinds of music
and the arts is widespread throughout the community. Amongst
the musical events of that year was the performance of an opera
called *The Loving of Etain.* The composer of its music plays with
one of the most Scottish of folk groups, The Whistlebinkies. On
the face of it, opera and folk music are strange bedfellows.

There is, in fact, no surprise that Eddie McGuire's interests
range so widely, that he sees nothing incongruous about following
an evening appearance on stage at a folk club with a morning in
his studio working on music for a ballet or a symphony. It is more
proof, if proof were needed, that the barriers between the different genres are well and truly down.

Eddie's first contact with music was within the family fold. His
father was heavily involved in a male-voice choir, the St. Mungo
Singers, whose repertoire, although largely Scottish, ranged far and
wide. Singalongs in the house were a regular feature, it being accepted that all present would contribute a solo. Such a request was too
much for the young Eddie who would flee the room when it was his
turn. Even today, after thousands of appearances on stage, he stead-
fastly refuses to sing solo. When rock and roll hit the scene it drove
out his acceptance of traditional music. A ukelele and a piano came

his way one Christmas and he found an early ability to compose little tunes. Entering secondary school, Eddie was given the opportunity to learn a musical instrument and chose the flute. It is because of this opportunity and the doors that were subsequently opened to him because of it, that he has always been such a vociferous supporter of free musical education for all. The flute seems to have taken over his life, composing as much as playing occupying the hours. Attendance at Glasgow Schools Orchestra courses gave him an appreciation of the contributions of other instruments. Rock and roll was now out, the classics were his interest. Having arrived at the decision to be a professional musician, at the age of 18, Eddie took off for London where for four years he would study at the Royal Academy of Music.

From London, Eddie moved to Sweden where he was to study composition for a further year. That country had an unexpected influence on him. The Swedes, in addition to their strong fiddle tradition, have an interest in the native music of other countries and he was forever bombarded with requests to play Scottish folk music. This brought it home to him that for more than ten years he had neglected Scottish music for input from the fields of America and the classics. He began to think more about the traditional music he had grown up with around the house and at the charity functions he had attended with his parents. Once back in Glasgow from Sweden he knew he had to explore his musical roots.

The Scottish folk music scene was stirring dramatically at this time and Eddie met up with some people known as The Whistle-binkies. Their music at that time was heavily drawn from America and Ireland and unusually, they included story-telling in their performances. It was basically a guitar and fiddle line-up. Eddie joined them and would play a full part in the character change that followed over the next five years or so. The group became authentically Scottish, building around the country's three main traditional instruments, the fiddle, the clarsach and the pipes. The drum was brought into play as was the flute and the concertina. The members were highly competent musicians, willing to experiment, and, as most held day-time jobs, were not under the same pressure as some other groups dependent on gigs to keep body and soul together. They started on the Folk Club circuit and playing at scattered folk festivals. Their reputation from then on would grow quickly.

Prominence came in 1976 when they recorded 'Banks of Sicily' on a compilation of Hamish Henderson's works. The record company, Claddagh of Dublin particularly liked their sound and, recorded the first of the five albums that would be put out under the Claddagh label.

This early period playing in the folk field must have been of tremendous importance to Eddie McGuire's work as a composer. His talents in this field were now recognised. In 1972 he had received a commission from James Durrant the viola soloist and conductor to write a solo viola piece. This piece, called 'Martyr', blended dramatic modern music with traditional folk material. It made its mark and brought him to national prominence as a composer. Other commissions were to follow. In 1976 he wrote his symphonic poem 'Calgacus' to which we shall return. His solo composition piece, 'Rant', won the competition, organised by the Society for the Promotion of New Music, to find the test piece for the 1978 Carl Flesch International Violin Competition.

Now with a new and very traditional Scottish sound the Whistlebinkies were to spread their wings. They were prominent at the annual Lorient Festival, toured in Germany and in 1976, rather unusually, took part in the Festival of Political Song held in the sector of Berlin controlled by East Germany.

The eighties saw a very busy Eddie McGuire. On top of regular appearances throughout Scotland the group went once or twice a year to the Continent to take part in festivals, experienced a winter tour in Sweden and his own playing included Burns Suppers in the USSR. He composed a number of pieces for solo instruments, wrote the suite, 'Inner Sound' which provided the background music for a documentary film (performed by The Whistlebinkies) and scored for 7:84 Theatre Company's dramatisation of Fionn McColla's novel, *The Albannach*. The landmark, if not the highlight, of the decade, though, was surely his provision of the music for Peter Pan. This he wrote at the request of the Scottish Ballet who seemed to like the idea of McGuire's mingling the Scottish with the modern. And as if to emphasise his inventiveness, he designed a new instrument played with a bow and based on that old music hall bit of dexterity, the musical saw. This ballet has been performed over a hundred times, and is included in the repertoire of companies as far away as the Hong Kong Ballet.

The decade of the nineties kicked off with The Whistlebinkies becoming the first Scottish folk group to tour in China. Back in

1974 Eddie had given a lecture on Chinese music and there is no doubt that some of the questions that came from the Chinese cultural revolution such as, 'who is Art for? the people or the elitist?' had caused him to think seriously as to the audience he wanted to write for. Around that time too he had been in discussions with the Professor of Chinese at Edinburgh University and said how wonderful it would be if a Scots music group could perform in China. While in Hong Kong, when his ballet was being performed, he had travelled to meet with some musicians in Beijing, and as a follow on to this meeting a Chinese folk group travelled to this country while in turn The Whistlebinkies made their historic tour. The group spent nearly three weeks in China and gave workshops as well as stage appearances in Canton, Shanghai and Beijing. With a feeling of travelling from the sublime to the ridiculous, the next year saw The Whistlebinkies perform at the Dark Days Festival in Iceland while a -20 degree blizzard raged outside the hall. A few years later the group returned to the Far East to play in Taiwan. The invitation to play at the very traditional festival that is Auchtermuchty's (organised by the Traditional Music and Song Association) obvi-

ously very much pleased Eddie McGuire and the group as it showed how they are regarded in the mainstream folk world. Another accolade was the rather surreal piece called 'Scottish Circus', written specially for The Whistlebinkies by the late American composer, John Cage.

In recent years The Whistlebinkies have switched to the recording services of Greentrax. There is a refinement to their playing. There is no taint of foreign rhythms. Their music still comes over as modern but within the

The Whistlebinkies

basic richness of the Scottish tradition. Everything they play is well thought out and makes full use of the skills and knowledge of superb musicians. Anyone looking for throbbing amplification should search elsewhere.

One commission which emphasises Eddie McGuire's international standing was the one given to him by the organisers of the Lorient Festival, perhaps the greatest of all Celtic music festivals, when he was asked to write the 1997 Festival's grand finale. This 50-minute piece, which he called 'The Celtic Epic', was performed by the Festival Orchestra complete with brass, woodwinds and strings, and brought together The Whistlebinkies, the Glasgow Skye Pipe Band, a Breton pipe band, a Breton bombarde ensemble, a Galician bagpipe soloist, an Irish piper, the Manx singer Emma Christian, and the Flint Male Voice Choir singing in Welsh. Even the carnyx, a bronze, boar-headed horn dating from pre-Christian times was included. This major work expressed the development of Celtic music over 2000 years, from its Eastern origins to the present day. 'The Celtic Epic' finished with a reel that Eddie had written on his first visit to Lorient some 20 years earlier.

Finally, let us remind ourselves that Eddie's symphonic poem, 'Calgacus', written in 1976, has not left the scene. It came to prominence again with its performance in 1997 when the piper of The Whistlebinkies joined the BBC Scottish Symphony Orchestra on the stage of the Albert Hall in London at one of the year's Promenade Concerts proving once again that the music and instruments of Scotland hold their own in any company. And the piper who strode the stage that night was the same Robert Wallace who had watched the first performance of 'Calgacus' from the balcony of the Bute Hall in Glasgow 21 years ago.

CHAPTER 5

The Fiddle and its Music

*I'm that fond o' my fiddle, I could
just sit in the inside o't an' look oot.*

– Peter Milne

THE ACT OF PROSCRIPTION of 1746 which followed the collapse of
the Jacobite cause was designed to bring the Highlanders to heel
by savaging their culture, to make them less of a race apart. It was
a largely successful ploy, removing the powerfully emotional bagpipe from the scene and demoralising a people by scheduling their
songs and dances for oblivion. Fortunately for us today, the Act
was to be repealed within some 40 years and though the scars
remained a vital culture did not die. But one of the interesting
results of the proscription of the bagpipe was that the door was
opened for the fiddle to become one of the national instruments of
Scotland, played from one end of the country to the other. A pipe
band may fit in with the picture of Scottish hills and glens and tartan, stirring the heart of visitor and native alike. The fiddle sees
the Scot at his own fireside or in concert or dance hall. It presents
a 'couthier' scene.

When we use the word fiddle today, we are of course talking
about a violin. It was not always so. We have long had a sentimen-
tal attachment to the word fiddle, but early fiddles were pretty
rough affairs. They were somewhat guitar shaped with flat backs
and fronts. There is the inevitable discussion about origin, not surprising when stringed instruments can be traced back to thousands
of years before the birth of Christ. Many accept the origins of
bowed instruments lie in the East. Some credit returning crusaders
with importing them to this country. Nearer home, the case for
something akin to a fiddle being an early indigenous Celtic instrument is propounded by the Irish. We turn to Thomas the Rhymer
who lived in the late 1200s for confirmation that stringed instruments, bowed, plucked and played with a plectrum, have long been
on the Scottish musical scene:

Harp and fedyl both he fande
The getern and the sawtry
Lut and rybid ther gon gan,
Thair was al maner of mynstralsy.

The mention of the harp, of course, is not unexpected. Its appearance on Pictish columns can be traced back to the eighth century. However, the well reported fiddling entertainment provided by the capital city's fiddlers for Mary Queen of Scots when she arrived here in 1560 lets us know that the fiddle had by then become a significant social fixture. The report is spoiled by the later knowledge that the sound was so abysmal Mary moved her bedroom to another part of Holyrood in case there should be a repeat performance.

The fiddle, though, was in the process of being ousted by the viol, James the Fifth normally being given credit for the introduction of that instrument. Slightly larger, superior in tone and fretted like a guitar, the viol's strings varied from three to six. It is interesting to find the viol came in various sizes. In addition to the treble viol, there was the tenor or viol de braccio, a bass viol da gamba and a double bass violone. So we see the beginnings of string ensembles. A 'chest of viols' containing six mixed instruments would in due course become a standard piece of furniture in many houses of pretension. A surprising amount of viol music has been unearthed in recent years.

The viol, then, appeared to have held sway until the arrival of the violin, the Scots clinging to their beloved word, fiddle. The Italians led the way in craftmanship, the family of Amati in Cremona as early as the beginning of the seventeenth century producing violins of legendary tone. And from the same town came Antonio Stradivari (1649-1737), the one violin-maker known to the man in the street. A reference book written around the turn of this century records £200 being paid for a Stradivarius, at a time when the cost of its raw materials was estimated at five shillings or 25 pence in today's currency. When these Italian violins reached us, Scottish fiddlers realised their superiority over the home-made product. In today's parlance, there was a market to be satisfied, and home fiddle makers started to copy these imports, developing an affinity for the violin of a particular Italian violin maker, selling their Scottish made instruments quite honestly as copies of a

Cremona or Amati or Ruggieri or whichever Italian violin maker had attracted their fancy. Austria too provided models for home fiddle-makers. Alexander Kennedy based his instruments on Jacob Stainer as did Ruddiman of Aberdeen (1733-1810) before taking Stradivari as his model. By the 1700s, Matthew Hardie had established his fame as a fiddle-maker and others were to follow in his train. In fact fiddle-makers became so prolific in Scotland that by the end of last century a whole host of books had been written about them.

A sizeable number of fiddlers today, gifted with their hands, turn their attention to the making of a fiddle. It is one of those things that looks straightforward but where success is difficult to achieve. It is difficult to appreciate the number of factors that interact when making such an instrument; the angle given to the arching, the relationship between the front and the back, the varnish and number of coatings all bear on the tone. Maple has long been one of the most popular woods used in fiddle making, especially for the back, sides and neck, with pine and spruce favoured for the front. Alexander Grant of Speyside, whose disc-shaped 'Rondello' fiddle is worth looking at in the Inverness museum, experimented with bog fir which he thought because of its great age produced a finer tone.

A musician benefits from access to music. Written music probably first came from the monasteries. Not unexpectedly the monks did not give their attention to jigs, reels and strathspeys. When one thinks of the pages and pages of music that are circulated around fiddlers today in advance of a rally, it is somewhat startling to recollect that at one time printed material was not available. For those not blessed with a good ear and a good memory, music had to be written and carried in some kind of pocket book. Not until the seventeenth century was printed music available. The Skene manuscript, which scholars date in the first quarter of the seventeenth century, contained and named some Scottish melodies. Then, prompting the suggestion that the Scottish king, now ruling an enlarged realm from London, had taken some real culture south with him, we find some Scottish airs included in Playford's *English Dancing Master* published in London in 1650. Playford continued to include Scottish tunes in his collections and a milestone was reached in 1700 when he published *A Collection of Original Scotch Tunes for the Violin.*

Publishers north of the border would now augment the music coming from London. Two comments on their music are worth making. First, this newly published music was essentially dance music. Second, although presented as fiddle music the German flute is often mentioned and bass parts given for the harpsichord and violincello. This prompts the reminder that in later years the 'cello (which displaced the viol da gamba in the early 18th century) was to be a standard backing instrument for fiddles playing for dancing and its virtual disappearance from such a scene represents a sad loss.

The first half of the eighteenth century saw a number of song and country dance books appear which included music for the fiddle, but we must wait until the second half of the century before books arrived on the scene clearly titled as collections of reels. In 1780 came Angus Cumming of Grantown's *Collection of Strathspeys or Old Highland Reels*. Two years earlier, 'Soldiers Joy' may have made its first appearance in print in Joshua Campbell of Glasgow's *Collection of the Newest and Best Reels and Minuets*. Campbell was reputedly a considerable guitarist but unfortunately we know nothing about any efforts he may have made to involve fiddle and guitar together.

As the eighteenth century drew to a close there was an explosion of fiddle music publications. And particularly we have to note the compositions of those seeking, if not careers, then pin money or part time employment as fiddlers and later as dancing teachers. What characters some of these early fiddlers were! Fife's Patie Birnie, who is said to have run all the way home without stopping from the Battle of Bothwell Bridge, kept body and soul together by playing in hostelries and on the ferry across the Forth. His money-making technique was first to apologise profusely to passengers for keeping them waiting for his arrival before producing his fiddle. To quote Ramsay:

And crave their pardon that sae lang
He'd been a-coming;
Syne his bread-winner out he'd bang
And fa' to bumming.

Birnie of course is supposed to have written 'The Auld Man's Mare's Deid' which appeared in the Scots Musical Museum of 1771.

Much better remembered than Birnie is James Macpherson, fiddler, composer and, regretably, freebooter. Macpherson was a kind of Robin Hood who, having fought his way from the clutches of the law once when due to be hanged, was recaptured and received his comeuppance at Banff. Prior to ascending the scaffold he composed his famous rant, and legend has it he was allowed to play this tune before the rope was placed around his neck.

Sae rantingly, sae wantonly,
Sae dauntonly gae'd he:
He play'd a spring, and danc'd it roun',
Below the gallows tree.

After playing Macpherson offered his fiddle to the crowd but no one would accept it. Disgusted, he broke the fiddle over his knee. A piece of the instrument can be seen today in the Clan Macpherson museum in Newtonmore.

Just as colourful as Macpherson, and a great deal more respectable, was the great Niel Gow of Inver, fiddler to four Dukes of Atholl and reckoned in his time to be a musician without equal in Scotland. Gow is important to our story as he moved fiddling away from being a purely amateur art and broke ground as a professional musician. Word of his talent spread around the aristocracy and demand for his services grew. Indeed, he seemed to become something of a cult figure. A special occasion demanded the presence of Niel Gow and this did not only apply in Scotland. London opened its doors to him and at least one major ball was postponed for a year so that the dancers might enjoy the music of Gow. The many references made to him in our literature ranging from the comments of the Lowland and less than wealthy Burns to the aristocratic Elizabeth Grant in her *Memoirs of a Highland Lady* suggest Gow had extensive fame and popularity. Many of his compositions are still widely played today. Some of his quotes like the following make us chuckle: 'Oh Mr. Gow', said the Duchess of Gordon, 'I've not been at all well lately; in the morning my head swims - a sudden giddiness comes over me'.

'Ah ken what ye mean, yer Ladyship', Gow replied, 'when ah've been fu' the nicht afore, it's like a haill bike of bees bizzin' in ma bonnet'.

Mrs. Lyon, the wife of the minister at Glamis, provided the words for Gow's great tune, 'Farewell to Whisky', and we remember too the words of Burns about Niel, some of which can be seen on the plaque which adorns the grey stone walls of his cottage:

Nae fabled wizard's wand I trow
Had e'er the magic art of Gow
When in a wave he draws his bow
Across his wondrous fiddle.

In brisk strathspey or plaintive air
What rival can wi' you compare
O' wha could think a hank o' hair
Could thus transform a fiddle!

Gow, of course, has come down to us through the world of art. Sir Henry Raeburn painted him four times and his portraits can be viewed in the National Portrait Gallery and in the ballroom of Blair Castle. It is generally agreed, too, that it is Gow who appears in David Allan's painting, 'Highland Dance', with his brother playing the 'cello.

Of Gow's four surviving sons, Nathaniel and Niel junior made the most musical impact. Nathaniel excelled his father as a composer with nearly 200 pieces to his credit. Many of his compositions such as 'Fairy Dance' and 'Caller Herrin'' are still well known today. A trumpeter to the sovereign, he had his financial ups and downs as owner of a music shop in Edinburgh, first at the North Bridge and later in Princes Street and Hanover Street. His shop advertisements offering guitars and mandolins show the range of instruments available to the public two centuries ago.

If Burns was to be kind about Niel Gow he was also to pay full tribute to another fiddler, William Marshall, perhaps the highest star in the firmament. Burns described him as, 'the first composer of strathspeys of the age' and used Marshall's 'Miss Admiral Gordon' as the setting for 'I Love My Jean' ('of a' the airts the wind can blaw'). Marshall, though, was different from Gow in many ways. A native of Fochabers in the County of Banff, he entered the service of the Duke of Gordon at an early age and remained with him all his working life. He was an interesting man with a wide range of interests outside music: clock-making, astrology and architecture all commanded his attention. His compositions possess quality and his 1822 *Collection of Scottish Airs, Melodies, Strathspeys and Reels* represents Scottish traditional music at its best. Unfortunately, some fiddlers take a step or two away from Marshall because of his use of flat keys and fondness for louping across the strings. Marshall we are told had little sympathy for those who found his tunes too difficult, advising them to practise more.

The last member of the triumvirate that any book on fiddles must include is of course Scott Skinner. James Scott Skinner was born in Banchory in 1843 into a very musical household. His father at that time was a gardener, but following an accident with a gun which took off three of his fingers (hence the name of Skinner's later composition, 'The Left-handed Fiddler') capitalised on his musical ability and changed occupations to become a dancing teacher. Yet Skinner would always acknowledge his brother Sandy as the first to take him in hand musically: 'I could not have been much more than six years of age when my brother Sandy took in hand to teach me the fiddle, and he was the most rigorous of taskmasters. Looking back on these days, I sometimes marvel that, when left to my own resources, a reactionary revulsion of feeling did not make me eschew the violin for all time. But, despite the grim school in which I was reared, my love for music, and particularly the music of my own country, was deep and innate and strong enough to survive the humiliating punishment I received because of my alleged lack of "glegness in the uptak".'

Because of the need to bring money into the house, the young Scott Skinner was also taught to vamp on the 'cello and soon found himself playing with brother Sandy at dances. Then around the age of eight or nine, Skinner went to play with (his expression is 'work for') Peter Milne when the engagements would frequently involve an eight or ten mile walk. But bearing in mind the reputation Skinner would eventually achieve, his comments on Milne have considerable interest: 'Peter Milne, in my opinion, was one of the grandest Strathspey players that ever graced Scotland, and probably the finest native musician of any country in the world. He was a genius and a great preserver of the finest of the old Scottish melodies, and a leader of the progressives amongst Strathspey exponents.'

Skinner would now take the road south to join a boys' orchestra known as Dr. Mark's Little Men and it was here he was to be given the classical violin training which would stand him in such good stead in the future. The orchestra, though, had its ups and downs, managing in one year to both play before Queen Victoria and busk for money in the streets.

Skinner returned north in his teens and after an apprenticeship period, sallied forth as a dancing teacher like his father. He seems to have made a reasonable living, won prizes for his dancing and included personnel on the Queen's estate at Balmoral amongst his pupils. He also formed a dance band which frequently included clarinet and cornet in its line-up, and played widely in the North of Scotland.

But a change was now in the offing. In 1893, Skinner was a member of a Scottish musical and dance group which toured America. He returned with a different vision of his future. He would now quit teaching dancing and become a concert violinist. The kilt became his adopted dress, his concert programmes a balance of the classics and Scottish traditional music. And this was to prove a successful recipe as the newspapers acclaimed his performances and the public responded by filling the halls where he was appearing.

Skinner had always had an interest in composing and had had some modest successes. But his 1881 Miller o' Hirn collection, followed some years later by his Logie collection, confirmed his place amongst our top composers. His later collections and individual pieces are still prominent today, and indeed it is uncommon to attend a Scottish music concert where something of his is not played. His compositions exceeded 600. We accept him as he titled himself, 'the Strathspey King'.

In the end Skinner influenced the playing quality of Scottish music, developed and clarified fiddle bowing in his compositions, and made people think about the influence of key on a tune. He was, we realise now, a genius.

So many fiddlers have given Scottish music so much it is impossible to name them all in a book of this size. Those of us who heard Hector Mac-Andrew play will long remember the experience. With the

Aly Bain in a session at Kinross Festival in the mid 70s

45

'Shetland Sound' now a prominent part of the music scene we express our gratitude to Tom Anderson, not only for his performances and compositions but for his dedication in bringing the music of his northern isles to its deserved and honoured place.

Yehudi Menuhin, one of the world's greatest violinists, has long been a good friend to Scottish fiddlers. Many will be acquainted with his comment: 'Their music knows no detour – it goes straight to our feet if dance we must, to our eyes if cry we must and always directly to our hearts evoking every shade of joy, sorrow or contentment. The genuine Scottish fiddler has an infallible sense of rhythm, never plays out of tune and is a master of his distinctive and inimitable style, which is more than can be said of most "schooled" musicians. We classical violinists have too obviously paid a heavy price for being able to play with orchestras and follow a conductor.'

CHAPTER 6

John Mason
and the
Scottish Fiddle Orchestra

I dwell amang the caller springs
That weet the Land o' Cakes,
And aften tune my canty strings
At bridals and late-wakes:
They ca' me Mirth.

"Leith Races" – **Robert Fergusson** (1750-1774)

Fidlers, your pins in temper fix,
And roset weel your fiddlesticks.

"The Daft Days" – **Robert Fergusson** (1750-1774)

APART FROM AMPLE GIRTH and eyes with a bit of the devil in them, the first thing one notices about John Mason is an accent that hails from northern parts. Although it is many years since he left Orkney (the Masons' roots were in Westray), the accent, so remarkably different from the Shetlanders, still filters through, albeit at some times stronger than others.

Music is much in evidence in Orkney family life and it is no surprise he talks about fiddle and town band playing relatives although the piano was his mother's choice of instrument. The family's tastes veered to the light classics. The toddler John, however, was to make an early discovery of traditional music. The war was in progress and his parents, to keep him out of mischief while they were involved in auxiliary work, allowed him to play with a hand-cranked gramophone. Two records came into his possession and these he played day in and day out, the old Beltona record of The Four Cameron Men playing the Circassian Circle and a recording of an Orkney fiddler, J. Johnston of Mirland playing some his own compositions. Within a few years, John would start to learn the fiddle under the eye of a relative, but, he recalls, it was pretty basic stuff. To another relative, but this time a more terrifying figure, he went for piano lessons, the emphasis being on scales and, Scottish music still being considered a bit *infra dig*, the light classics. The one Scottish piece he was allowed to play created a hunger for more.

In his early teens, his father's work necessitating a move, the family uprooted from Orkney and travelled the length of the country to Wigtown. It was not, John found, to be compared with Orkney in music terms, but country dance music was beginning to come to the fore and he was allowed to sit in at practices and play his fiddle with the local dance band run by Jack Dunlop. This, he recalls, helped him wonderfully to get up the necessary speed in his playing. As he matured he played both fiddle and piano with some bands, but on leaving home to study law at Edinburgh University, he responded to his father's advice to leave his fiddle behind in case it interfered with his studies. His academic progress must have been more than adequate for within a couple of years his father relented and John was again playing regularly, first for the University dancers and then, meeting some fellow Orcadians, forming a group known as the Mason-Stewart Country Dance Band. It didn't quite set the heather on fire, their most prestigious engagement being the spot playing during the intervals of the bingo sessions in Leith! To mask their limited repertoire, the tunes were played in a different sequence every night. No one ever seemed to notice.

Now legally qualified, John accepted a position in Newton Stewart. Almost immediately, he became friendly with a couple who were to have a considerable influence on his musical life. Mona and Bobby Stewart were not only highly talented musicians, but through their respective fathers (one had been a pipe major and the other an enthusiast for music history as well as a prominent fiddler) the couple had absorbed a huge knowledge of Scottish traditional music. John now started to interest himself seriously in the traditional idiom and the Stewarts were willing teachers. He joined the Stewarts' country dance band, learned to play guitar and clarinet and kept his link going with the Wigtown Burgh Band he had played with earlier. These years in Newton Stewart meant that he got to know the capabilities of a large number of instruments, enhanced his stage experience and built up a store of tunes and a knowledge of Scottish music and composers. The debt he owes to the Stewarts, he has never forgotten.

In 1967, John married an Orcadian girl and shortly afterwards they set up home in Troon where he was now to practise law. A fiddle grapevine seemes to have operated and before long he was ensconced in the Kilmarnock Strathspey and Reel Society and there played happily for a number of years. A number of the members of that society, had been at one time members of the defunct Land Of Burns Strathspey and Reel Society and were keen to see the return of a society to Ayr. The wheels were set in motion and in 1972 the Ayr and Prestwick Strathspey and Reel Society came into being with John Mason as conductor. The Kilmarnock Society showed every kindness to the musical fledgling, including providing it with music. It is worth recording that when the Kilmarnock conductor, Andrew Fulton, died, John wrote a remembrance piece of music for him called 'Nature's Gentleman'. This was taken up by the writer Harry Barry, became the song 'Lochinver' and was recorded by Valerie Dunbar.

While fiddlers' rallies are common enough events today, their history is not that long. It was in 1970, when the Mod was due to be held in Oban, that the conductor and secretary of the Oban and Lorne Strathspey and Reel Society came up with the idea of collecting all the competitors together for a public concert in the Corran

John Mason

Hall on the Saturday evening. For this, somebody in the television world coined a new name; they called it a Fiddlers' Rally.

Now the Mod, though a showpiece of Gaeldom, was not given to travelling below the Highland Line. At that time, the President of An Commun Gaidhealach was the Reverend Archie Beaton, the minister at Dundonald, and he was enthusiastic about bringing the Mod out of the Highlands to Ayr. This was accomplished in 1973 and the Ayr and Prestwick Society was given the responsibility by the Mod committee of arranging the traditional fiddlers' rally. The note of sadness attached to this event was, of course, that the Reverend Archie Beaton did not live to see his dream reach fruition. Let it be said here that when John Mason wrote 'Lament for the Death of the Reverend Archie Beaton', he wrote without doubt one of our finest slow airs. The television coverage of the Mod rally considerably encouraged the public's interest in such events. Perhaps the big breakthrough was that John along with some others was able to persuade a record company to bring out a long-playing record of the rally. Looking back it seems incredible that that LP was the first ever recording of massed fiddles.

The Ayr and Prestwick Society soon settled down to a steady round of engagements but another 'first' was looming. The committee of the Silver Broom contest, the curling competition which takes place between Scotland and Canada, asked the Society to arrange a rally to take place in Perth during the time of the competition. This is thought to be the first rally ever to take place, unconnected with the Mod.

The rally fuse had now been lit, the public appetite whetted and other societies followed suit. In 1978 John was approached by the fund-raiser of Cancer Research with the suggestion that he organise such an event in London. It seems to have been a challenge he was unable to refuse. To use his phrase, 'the Fiery Cross was sent round the Societies'. There was a superb response and the occasion in the Albert Hall exceeded all expectations. This was the event that led to the birth of the Scottish Fiddle Orchestra. The name 'Fiddlers' Rally' had been used in London to explain the event though the Southrons associated the word rally with motor bikes, and it was after the Cancer Research concert that the idea of a national orchestra was firmed up. Musicians from all over Scotland were now meeting regularly at rallies. Inevitably, pre-concert practice was, as it still is today limited. A national orchestra, it was thought, could arrange regular practices throughout the year, and, what was equally important, offer additional large scale Scottish musical entertainment in the country's largest halls. It cannot be said that John Mason's view of what was needed in Scotland in musical terms met with everyone's approval. What is certain is that the impact of the SFO both within and outwith Scotland, and the work it has done in the promotion of Scottish music outwith our boundaries, has brought pleasure to tens of thousands of exiles and helped to keep the name of Scotland alive in commercial markets. And let us not forget the immense amount of money the Scottish Fiddle Orchestra has raised for a wide range of charities.

1980 saw the Orchestra start with a 150 members. All instruments except brass were accepted. The initial rota of concerts was set at the Music Hall in Aberdeen, the Caird Hall in Dundee, Edinburgh's Usher Hall, the City Hall in Glasgow and the Royal Albert Hall in London. These prominent concerts brought an invitation from Scottish Television to perform a series for the channel and this was followed by a similar offer from Channel 4. Many other television appearances such as the Hogmanay Shows were to follow. There is no doubt these performances resulted in the up and coming generation showing much more interest in Scottish music, and fiddle playing in particular, than before.

Dallas in Texas provided an unusual venue for the SFO but Blenheim Palace provided the better story. During the playing of 'The Hen's March Over The Midden', one of the 'roadies' dressed as a pantomine hen (perhaps copying a certain conductor) wiggled his derriere to the music whereupon one of the guard dogs nearly succeeded in taking a lump out of it. India was added to the venue list, a group going out to take part in a Burns celebration every January. St. Andrew's Night also sees some of the orchestra in action in the Middle East. On their general concert circuit, Birmingham has replaced Dundee, and York and Inverness have been added.

Never slow in responding to change, John Mason early on took the SFO into the video market. The first video, 'Northern Lights', was an immediate success and eight videos have been made so far including 'Over the Water' which covers their concerts in both Northern Ireland and the Republic. These videos have received wide circulation and high acclaim through the Public

Broadcasting Stations TV link up in the States. Indeed one friend of a member of the orchestra complained that his 'away from it all' holiday in Florida had nearly been ruined as every time he switched on the TV he saw the SFO. But it was largely as a result of the videos being shown in North America that the invitation came in for a major tour in Canada. This tour seems to be entering the world of legend. Tickets for all the concerts were sold out months in advance and the orchestra received rapturous welcomes. As one member put it. 'For the first time in my life I received a standing ovation without playing a note.' But crisis is seldom far away from any extended tour and this tour was no exception. One story is worth telling. The members flying from Glasgow, including John, arrived in Vancouver to discover their luggage (containing their tartan stage wear) had gone astray. Canadian Airlines in a damage limitation exercise kitted out the men with black trousers, white shirts, bow ties and black shoes for the first concert but it would have been unthinkable for the conductor not to appear in a kilt. One Edinburgh flight member of approximate girth to John volunteered to loan John his highland attire but unfortunately had feet the size of helicopters. The conductor wielded his baton at that first concert with shoes threatening to take off at every movement and only kept fastened to his feet by the laces.

The most moving concert, he claims, was played in Vancouver on Canada Day. After he had expressed the wish, 'Happy Birthday, Canada' from the stage the audience rose to sing 'O Canada'. It was one of these special electric moments when the atmosphere can be felt. The tour reached a climax at the last concert in Toronto. There, in the magnificent setting of the Molson Amphitheatre, the Scottish Fiddle Orchestra played to an audience that exceeded 10,000. The video of that concert is being widely shown across North America and looks set to be the orchestra's best seller.

No comment on John Mason is complete without reference to his compositions. His 'Ceud Mille Failte' (A Hundred Thousand Welcomes) starts many a programme throughout the land, and 'Archie Beaton' has become a much loved slow air. John started composing while still a teenager and has not forgotten his northern roots with pieces like 'The Shetlander', 'The Orcadian' and 'The Hardanger Fiddle'. But his output broadened when he started conducting, when he had the vehicle at hand, so to speak, to have his many arrangements and compositions performed. One suspects he has a soft spot for 'The Wild Rose of the Mountain'. This descriptive piece was taken by Harry Barry and turned into the song 'Scotland Again'. Those who have heard Anne Lorne Gillies' or Mary Sandeman's recordings of it will remember its fine chorus of 'Caledonia, Caledonia'. There is growing fancy amongst musicians for his recent 'Flower of Portencross'. John has ventured into describing poetry musically with his 'Tam O' Shanter' and 'Cutty Sark' overture, his overture tribute to the '45 Rising, 'Prince of the Mists' and his Burns Cantata for Reader, Mezzo-Soprano, Tenor and Orchestra, 'Til a' the Seas Gang Dry', which lasts for 45 minutes. He is generous in his response to orchestras seeking permission to play his compositions.

John is full of praise for the young fiddle players of today. He tends to classify them as following the Scottish classical style or what he calls the brilliant 'Aly Bain' style. A frequent judge at the Glenfiddoch Fiddle Championships held annually at Blair Castle, he describes today's young players as 'terrifying' in their ability. Within the SFO he has gathered some young players into what he calls 'the folk symphony' and often brings them on to play towards the end of a concert where their hard driving rhythm has tremendous appeal.

With the SFO's membership drawn pretty well from the length and breadth of Scotland, inevitably having been reared on different playing styles, it is interesting to ask John if this leads to any particular problems. His answer is no. He does acknowledge he has sometimes to struggle to get 'lift', since old Scots tunes, he says, cannot all be played at the same speed and every melody, he believes, demands a tempo and rhythm of its era.

In 1987 John was privileged to attend Buckingham Palace to be presented by Her Majesty the Queen with the MBE for his services to music and charity. That was an event which he will never forget.

CHAPTER 7

Dougie MacLean

Hey! for the music o' Baldy Bain's fiddle
Redd up the barn, an' we'el gie ye a reel.

The Barn Dance – W D Cocker

EVEN BEFORE MEETING Dougie MacLean, one is aware of his one-ness with his surroundings: his music, songs and interviews have seen to that. His opening comments tell you he is the third gener-ation to have roots around Dunkeld. He lives in the old school he and his father attended. It not only includes his studio; it is his spiritual anchor.

Hamlet life means much making of home entertainment and the

MacLean house was no exception. His mother played the melodeon and his father the fiddle. Both instru-ments he was encouraged to lift and experiment with so that at an early age he was playing by ear. He recalls in his teens buying a mandolin for his father's birthday one year and being able to sit playing it in the bus on the way home. At village func-tions he both sang and listened to the music of the great country dance bands like The Hawthorne, Ian Powrie's and Jim Cameron's that became legends in their lifetimes. He has no doubt that growing up with Scottish music and getting to know so many tunes intimately at an early age gave him a flying start in his musical career. At secondary school in Blairgowrie he first formed a duo before making up a group called Puddocks Well. It must have been quite a group, as it included others who would make a name for themselves in the music field like Andy M. Stewart and Martin Hadden who, in the fullness of time, joined Silly Wizard. The group became regulars at Blairgowrie Folk Club. Early gigs included the inevitable Rurals and playing for skiers at a local hotel.

From school Dougie was bound for a career in civil engineering. He confesses to not being a good student, allowing music to pull him away from his studies. One day in the street a friend drew up in a van and approached him. 'His group', he explained, 'were taking off the next week to play in Germany and their fiddle player couldn't make the trip. Would Dougie like to join them?' Being a canny Scot he asked for five minutes to think it over. His reply of course came in the affirmative. The name of the group was The Tannahill Weavers.

So Dougie MacLean, at the age of 20, was introduced to the harsh realities of the touring life. The material of The Tannahill Weavers, who of course built a sizable reputation, was essentially Scottish, but put over in a much less formal way than would have been expected, say, in the country's variety theatres. There was no dress code, bothy ballads and reels rubbed shoulders with the songs of Tannahill and Burns, old books were scoured for material. It is worth while remembering that outside of folk clubs, such groups were not in great demand in Scotland at the time. The public was a bit reserved. It was a period of hippies and protest marches and to many a bit of subversiveness wasn't all that far away from the folk scene. Changes in the music scene on the Continent however, were opening up opportunities for folk artistes. European countries, especially Germany and Holland, had a long tradition of jazz clubs and, as interest in jazz waned, these clubs started to open up their premises for a night or two a week to other music forms. The Irish were not slow to move in and of course the experimentation with new sounds was underway. Bouzoukis and a range of instruments hitherto virtually unknown were now to be seen on stage and ways had been found to merge the playing of fiddles and pipes, a discovery that opened up a whole new world of sound.

Dougie had always been a bit of a singer and during his latter years with The Tannahill Weavers he became more prominent, both as a singer and song arranger. At a time when the vinyl output of folk groups was not significant, he recorded 'Are Ye Sleeping Maggie?' which brought at least his fiddle to the attention of a wider audience. Perhaps its reception was another factor in the decision he was now making to further his musical career.

He is quite positive he knew he was not going to achieve complete fulfilment as musician until he was performing his own material. Interpreting and arranging the music of others was only a step towards his final goal. The die being cast, he took the decision to leave The Tannahill Weavers. The parting was amicable.

With a partner, Dougie now returned to the European circuit, playing at all the major festivals. He accepted an invitation from his old friends in Silly Wizard to join them on an American tour before returning to the European venues where he was now so well known. Lying on a beach in France one day, feeling the pull of homeland, he drafted out a song he called Caledonia. It was included in an album of that name which was to receive a very good press. Shortly afterwards he made an album with Alex Campbell, a highly regarded singer in the sixties whom Dougie remembers with the greatest of affection. Indeed it was largely on Campbell's advice that Dougie would later form his own recording company.

Dougie's penetration into the North American market has been, rather like his career at home, a case of steady progress over the years. The province of Alberta in Canada gave him his first solo engagements, playing in the Peace River country at temperatures of around 40 below and in such places as Medicine Hat or thriving Edmonton with its large quota of exiles. Soon Australia and New Zealand would be added to his tours, but two important, one should say extremely important, happenings are worth recording. He established a home for himself amongst the Perth-shire hills where his heart had always been. And after one of the quickest courtships on record, he married his wife, Jenny. Jenny is a talented artist who applies an individual style to her landscapes and designs the covers for his CDs. Appropriately, they met at an Art Centre where Dougie was performing. Coming from a musical family her-self, one suspects she convinced him he had all the necessary talents to be a success and encouraged him to follow his own beliefs. And she endorsed his decision to form his own record company. One must remember it is one thing to make a recording, another to have it distributed and sold. Business is business and the record companies will obviously concentrate on what they think will bring in the profits, which is not necessarily the music an artiste wants to record. His first venture, though, with his own company, Dunkeld Records, titled 'Craigie Dhu', sold well and the company was on its way.

From here on, Dougie MacLean's story becomes a series of major milestones. During 1989-90, in a series of concerts, he played to over 50,000 people in the States, including a sell-out concert in New York City Town Hall. Then came his musical involvement with Kathy Mattea, one of the biggest ever names in the country music field in the States. Succumbing to the simple singing and playing style of Dougie on 'Craigie Dhu', she sought him out when he came to play in Nashville. They soon discovered they had much in common, wanting to put over their own messages in their songs. They have worked much together over the years, the two families becoming friends and visiting each other regularly. Mattea included Dougie's song 'Ready for the Storm' in one of her albums; they have appeared together in 'Celtic Connections', the BBC filmed 'Transatlantic Sessions' and of course in 'Song Roads', a musical journey from Nashville to Dunkeld' which was filmed for BBC 2.

Many people who don't follow the folk scene came to know about Dougie MacLean through, of all things, a beer advert. Fifteen years earlier he had, as already mentioned, expressed his homesickness in 'Caledonia'.

I've been telling old stories, singing songs
That make me think about where I come from
And that's the reason why I seem so far away today.

Tennents (part of the Bass conglomerate) wanted to use it in a beer commercial which depicted a young Scot quitting the rat race in London and returning north, the final shot showing him enjoying a drink in an Edinburgh pub. Initially he was against the idea of his song being used by a commercial organisation, but changed his mind when he saw how the commercial was structured. 'I didn't reckon it was just about selling beer,' he says. 'I saw it was about Scottish self-confidence'. In later years he would sing the song at Murrayfield before 65,000 people prior to a Welsh-Scotland rugby match. Caledonia of course is the name the Romans gave to that large part of Scotland they did not conquer, and is a name with an emotional appeal to Scots:

Let me tell you that I love you
And I think about you all the time
Caledonia, you're calling me
And now I'm going home.

In 1993 television viewers had the opportunity to see Dougie MacLean at home when BBC Television showed a special programme about him, *The Land - Songs of Dougie MacLean.*

Dougie has of course written music especially for the media and the theatre and special events such as the Loch Ness exhibition. His most famous piece in this connection must be 'The Gael' which was used by 20th Century Fox as the background music in their film *The Last of the Mohicans* based on Fenimore Cooper's book of that name. The tune has also become well known to visitors to the Edinburgh Tattoo where it has been played many times.

One could go on and on about Dougie MacLean's successes as a song-writer and artiste: his appearances at Carnegie Hall in New York and the the Australian National Festival in Alice Springs, (he plays a mean didgeridoo), an audience of 1,500 in Anchorage, Alaska, the BBC Television Hogmany show and his solo concert at the Festival Hall in Glasgow during the Celtic Connections Festival. 1997 saw him undertake five sell-out tours. The wonder is that he is so untainted as a person by it all. He remains devoted to his family and the music that calls to him from his Perthshire hills.

CHAPTER 8

Hamish Moore

For I'm a piper tae my trade
My name is Rab the Ranter,
The lasses loup as they were daft,
When I blaw my chanter.

"Maggie Lauder" – *Traditional song*

THE PLAYING OF THE bagpipes was forbidden under the 1746 Act of Proscription. One of the side-effects of the Act, it has been claimed by some, was that it encouraged the playing of the small pipes since they made less noise and could be played indoors, a reason some devotees refer to them as *parlour pipes*. Thus was hindered the zeal of any Redcoats bent on eradicating the culture of the Gaels. Whether that be fact or legend need not concern us, but it does suggest that the small pipes were being played in the Highlands over two centuries ago. Of course, the formation of the Highland Regiments to serve the Hanoverian cause and the repeal of the Act meant a huge need for pipers with their Highland pipes, a demand which all but removed the small pipes from the Highland scene. In the Lowlands they had a life of their own. That the small pipes have come to play such a prominent part in the contemporary music scene is due very largely to the skill and enthusiasm and willingness to break down barriers of pipers like Hamish Moore, Gordon Mooney and Rab Wallace and many members of the Lowland and Borders Pipers Society.

Hamish Moore's roots are in Glasgow and the Highlands. The son of a piper, he was motivated towards the pipes at an early age. Fortunately, his school possessed a pipe band and practice with it was topped up with additional instruction from an enthusiastic teacher who gave him individual lessons for two years on a daily basis. This teacher, Jack Crichton by name, was pipe major of Knightswood Juvenile Band in Glasgow, a feeder for existing Grade 1 bands at that time. The young Hamish became a member which gave him an introduction into the band and individual playing competition fields, although, he confesses, he did not feel at home in the competition arena.

From school, Hamish pursued his career intention of becoming a veterinary surgeon and studied at Edinburgh University's Royal Dick Veterinary School. The pipes though were not forgotten. He became involved in playing for the New Scotland Dancers, the University's country dance society, both at home and at dance festivals in Europe, quickly appreciating the need for consistency of rhythm in this kind of playing. After graduating, though, he found the work of a vet in the North of Scotland offered little free time for pursuing piping and his set of pipes seldom saw the light of day for a number of years.

Hamish was now to take up an appointment with the Ministry of Agriculture in Inverness and with reduced evening and week-end work a return to piping became possible. But prior to taking up this appointment he was to spend a happy ten weeks as a locum in County Clare in Ireland. The impact that Irish music, played on its home ground, made on him, was profound. Here he encountered music far removed from the competition field, music played purely for the pleasure of the piper and those around him. And here he encountered at close quarters the Uillean pipes, not only capable of being played indoors, but inherently compatible with other instruments.

Life has a funny way of producing surprises. Our paths are directed so often by chance. Hamish returned to Kingussie fired with enthusiasm about small pipes and made plain his feelings to a neighbour, John MacRae, who hailed from Kintail and who was likewise a piper. This gentleman said nothing, but the following morning quietly de-posited on the Moore's kitchen table a set of small pipes. He had, he said, inherited them from his father. They were dated late 19th century. Hamish arranged to have the pipes restored and a small chanter made by Colin Ross of Whitley Bay. Now equipped, he started to play with local folk musicians, showing how the small pipes could be made to blend with guitar, fiddle and concertina. Even at this time, Hamish recalls, he saw the worldwide possibilities of an instrument that was harmonically rich, portable and needed little maintainance. With the help of his father, who had an interest in wood turning, he experimented in the making of small pipes. He became ever more excited and enthusiastic about the potential of the instrument as other folk groups began flirting with large and small pipes in their line-up, and also as he began to receive enquiries for the pipes he was making.

In 1985 he accepted Dougie McLean's invitation to record an

album on Dougie's Dunkeld Records label. This album, *Cauld Wind Pipes,* was highly acclaimed and opened the minds of many to the potential of the small pipes. The following year, as a result of a recommendation given by Cathal MacConnel of the Boys of the Lough to an American music agent, he toured the States with the Ayrshire clarsach player, Katie Harrigan, a tour which was hugely successful. It was not to be wondered that in 1986 he made the decision to quit the veterinary field to play and make small pipes. He moved south to Dunkeld and set up his workshop. While playing most of the time in a solo capacity, he found time to perform frequently with three former members of Jock Tamson's Bairns, Ian Hardie, Rod Patterson and John Croall. But increasingly he became involved in teaching and the setting up of schools, starting off first in his own locality. These would be followed shortly by summer schools in West Virginia, California, North Carolina and Vermont. The Edinburgh International Folk Festival then commanded his attention, where he initiated and integrated the Piping Festival within the overall Festival.

While at a recording session for one of Billy Kay's *Odyssey* programmes in 1987, quite by chance Hamish encountered Dick Lee, the remarkable jazz saxophonist and clarinetist, who was also involved in providing incidental music for the programme. Trying out the combination of pipes and saxophone they were both struck by the possibilities afforded by this completely new junction of sounds. They started touring together and made two albums which received rave reviews. Here was confirmation, if it were needed, that the pipes need not be contained within musical boundaries. As Hugh MacDiarmid would later say in the Edinburgh *Evening News*: 'For giving the pipes a life divorced from their kilt and heather image, the man deserves a medal'.

Hamish Moore

Yet Hamish was in many ways to return to Scottish roots. 1993 saw him teaching at the Gaelic College in Cape Breton, Nova Scotia. He had particularly wanted to visit Cape Breton, that somewhat remote piece of land which had become home to so many Gaelic speaking Highlanders who had felt the wrath of the clearances. In the remoteness of Cape Breton he realised how easy it was for the culture these early settlers had brought with them to remain virtually unchanged. He found the speaking of Gaelic, the use of mouth-music *(port-a-beul)*, the old forms of dancing, especially step-dancing and Scotch reels, piping and fiddling to be completely normal facets of everyday life in Cape Breton today.

Prior to this visit, Hamish had had many meetings and discussions with Cape Breton fiddlers, especially Buddy MacMaster. These fiddlers were playing regularly for step-dancing, still the commonest form of dancing on the Island, and it was apparent they had a feeling for rhythm and interpretation of music that was not common in Scotland.

This first visit then made him aware of what had been lost from Scotland. How he would have loved to have visited Cape Breton years earlier when contact with a prior generation, with all that might have offered, would have been possible. He did make contact with one very old piper, Alec Currie, whose playing style had been handed down father-to-son from the emigrant days. His playing was completely devoid of influence by modern competition playing or by any other sources. The two pipers have obviously established a special relationship.

Hamish Moore's quiet demeanour can only conceal for so long the passion he feels about bringing the treasures of the past back to life in Scotland. The last hundred years and more he believes have seen Scottish culture both sanitised and standardised to fit perceptions of what that culture should be. Cape Breton, which he has now visited nine times, not only to teach but to spend time with those like Alec Currie, has entered his soul to a remarkable degree. Here is how he articulates the Cape Breton position:

'Scottish music in Cape Breton has remained very closely linked with the Gaelic language and the old Scottish step dancing, these two forces dictating and anchoring the tempos and rhythms of the music. Without these anchors, the music is free to change, and these changes in Scotland have been rapid and radical as a result of external influences.'

Hamish Moore believes that two major influences have affected our musical culture; first, the establishment of Highland Regiments and the introduction of piping competitions. These two phenomena have changed piping to such an extent that it is hardly recognisable as the same art form. The adoption of the pipes by the army, and the way they are played for martial purposes, has meant the pipes have become a military rather than a folk tradition. Competitions, of course, by their nature, produce the need for standard settings of music, a notion that is alien to other folk traditions in the world. The other principal result of competitions has been to increase the complexity of the technique which then becomes the dictating force on the tempos and rhythms of the music, rather than the natural rhythms of the dance and language being enhanced by subtly placed and executed ornaments.

Hamish Moore also expresses a strong view on what he calls the 'Victorianisation of Scotland'. He believes that quasi-classical influences have been imposed on Scottish music to make it fit for the drawing rooms of Edinburgh and London rather than the kitchen of the croft house. A conversation with Hamish Moore then, is not likely to be dull.

A look at some of Hamish's achievements since he entered the music field full time is sufficient to indicate his tremendous energy. Since 1986 he has toured North America 14 times and New Zealand twice. He has toured in Russia and worked with the Hungarian band, Vasmalom, and an Appalachian dance troupe. He has performed at festivals from Hong Kong to Philadelphia, taught at Summer Schools, made five albums, appeared numerous times on television and radio and played with members of the Montreal Symphony Orchestra. Additionally, he has taken part with Mairi Campbell and Dave Francis (currently director of Edinburgh Folk Festival) and Jean and Ryan MacNeil from Cape Breton in two Scottish tours of 'Welcome Nova Scotia' which tells how traditional Scottish music left our shores at the time of the Clearances and is now returning home.

Today Hamish Moore's concentration is on the manufacture of bellows-blown pipes. His work in the States over the years has provided dividends in that many of the orders he receives come from North America. His full life includes working on ways to improve the sound of the pipes by researching improvements in reed design. With his sons he seeks to promote the old style of piping. He has clocked up three years' service as chairman of the Lowland and Border Pipers' Society. With the help of Proiseact nan Ealan, he has established the highly successful Ceolas Summer School in South Uist, which teaches pipes, fiddle, step dance, Scotch reels and Gaelic song. The tutors are internationally renowned and come from Gaelic-speaking Scotland and Cape Breton. The declared aim of the school is to re-establish the close links between music, the Gaelic language and the rhythms of the old Scotch step dancing.

And if it does not seem too sacreligious a disclosure, Hamish Moore is developing some prowess as a fiddler.

CHAPTER 9

Cathy-Ann MacPhee

Gone are the kindest of people
Their joys their songs their ceilidhs
Where their homes were
Now deer run.

"*Luchd Na Beurla*" - **Mairi Mhor**

IN LOWLAND SCOTLAND, there is a measure of confusion about the culture of the Gael. There is a recognition that some songs carry the tag Heroic Ballads and have come down through the years from either the poets attached to the house of a chief, or some lesser being, but essentially a male. Then there are the work songs, consciously or unconsciously associated with women, where verse is followed by chorus. Film-makers love the waulking song where it makes good camera to show a group of ladies diligently beating in unison a length of wet home-woven cloth on a table as part of the shrinking process. Most Lowlanders too will tell you that a ceilidh was a gathering where story-telling and recitation joined song and music and was well removed from what is known today as ceilidh dancing from the North of England upwards.

In the world of song, especially, there is uncertainty. It is difficult to relate the singing in church of metrical psalms to the *port-a-beul*. And what does the Lowlander make of Marjorie Kennedy-Fraser, revered by some for saving Hebridean songs from extinction, castigated by others who either did not think them lost, or did not appreciate what she did to them. Again, many who thrill to the music of a march, say, played on the big pipes, cannot perceive what is involved in the playing of a piobaireachdd. Yet, long before there was a swell of interest in the Celtic world, the songs of the Gaels commanded goodwill throughout the country. The Mod was widely listened to or watched. But the few singers from Gaeldom who made national impact did so because they sang in English with the occasional lapse into Gaelic to inject authenticity into their performance. Things have changed over the past few years.

The folk/rock group Runrig, capturing the spirit of younger

generations, built up an international following by playing their native music in a very modern idiom. Capercaillie, with their highly polished performances, have penetrated the defences of older generations. It is time now to look at the contribution of a singer, who from her Hebridean base has broken new ground on behalf of Gaeldom.

Catherine-Ann MacPhee was born on the small outer isle of Barra. She did not take long to test her voice in public. By the age of five she was taking part in local ceilidhs. And a favourite way of passing time during stormy evenings on the island was to sing and dance for whoever was looking after her, but only after she had made sure the performance would culminate in the presentation of a bouquet.

When she was ten the family moved to Blackpool. Her father was serving in the Merchant Navy at the time and the move meant the family could spend more time together. The discovery her school music-teacher's name was also Catherine Ann (which meant she must be a nice person), was enough inducement for her to join the school choir. And so Cathy-Ann's first major appearance as a soloist in public was at the age of 13 when she appeared at a school concert in the famous Winter Gardens in Blackpool. Of that appearance in front of nearly a thousand parents and friends she remembers two

Cathy-Ann MacPhee

things. First, she enjoyed the experience, not being the slightest bit nervous; second, the song she sang was 'Yellow Bird Up High In Banana Tree'. Then, with her sixteenth birthday behind her, the family moved back to Barra.

Her desire for some kind of career on the stage seems to have strengthened as she got older and in the late seventies she auditioned for and was accepted by a new theatre initiative. Called Fir chlis (Northern lights) it was to become the first professional Gaelic theatre company. The spread of the population in the Highlands and Islands meant the cast had to adapt to the touring life and for nearly four years Cathy-Ann travelled widely from the company's base on Harris over much of the Highlands and Islands. Performances, of course, were in Gaelic, but full houses could be obtained on their occasional visits to places like London and Edinburgh. The theatre's productions were written especially for it by Gaelic writers and covered comedy, tragedy and pantomine. Her favourite tour, she remembers, was with Sean O' Casey's *Shadow of a Gunman*. It lost, she reckons, none of its power through translation into Gaelic. Her singing voice though seems to have been noticed by the powers that be. Generally there was a song worked in for her to sing in the production, or, failing that, a recording of her voice on tape was played during the interval break. Unfortunately, such touring companies depend to an extent on grants and when the inevitable cut came the company was forced to close down. Cathy-Ann looked around for another job.

The late Bobby Macleod of Mull was revered in music circles. Piper, accordionist, character, owner of the Mishnish Hotel in Tobermory and a one time Provost of the town, Bobby was one of Scotland's greatest ever band-leaders. Cathy-Ann's sister had married Bobby's bass-playing son, Alisdair, and through this connection Cathy-Ann made for Tobermory to take up a job in the hotel. And it was while working there she received a telephone call from John MacGrath of the 7:84 Theatre Company. MacGrath, who had seen Cathy-Ann perform in Edinburgh, invited her to join his company. She confessess to swithering over acceptance. The reason, she explains, was that she had never acted on stage speaking English, all her performances had been in Gaelic and the thought of having to put a character across in another language frightened the daylights out of her. But eventually she responded to John MacGrath's confidence in her and joined the company. 7:84 provided opportunities for travel and she took part in productions in Germany, Canada, America and Russia. A fond memory from her Russian tour is the evening in a hotel in Georgia which started off when a debonair gentlemen at a nearby table sent a bottle of champagne over to her. Conversation not unnaturally ensued. A bond was established as the Georgians explained how they (like the Gaels) were struggling to keep their language alive. As a bonus, they were keen to sing and the evening warmed up into a cracking ceilidh, right there in the dining room.

All the time 7:84 was bringing song more into its productions and Cathy-Ann increasingly found herself cast in roles where she was required to sing. She certainly had no thoughts of becoming a recording artiste at this time, but a little connivance was going on in the background between John MacGrath and Ian Green of Greentrax Records. In September of 1987, shortly after she had appeared in 7:84's television production *There is a Happy Land,* her first album, *Canan Nan Gaidheal* (The Language of the Gael) was recorded. The songs in it were fairly straightforward, *port-a-beul,* waulking, rowing and so on. It was a safe mix for somone not yet terribly well-known, and tastefully backed by some members of Ossian. The media received it well, critics in the States in particular noting the strength and the emotion of her voice. It was shortly after this, when singing at a ceilidh at Sleat in Skye, that Cathy-Ann got involved in a conversation with a very distinguished looking and elegant gentleman. On discovering she was due to return to Glasgow the next day, he insisted she travel with him on his private jet. She thought he was joking but he turned out to be Prince Frederick, the Queen of Denmark's husband. She accepted the lift.

Now married, Cathy-Ann said goodbye to the actress's life. Her last appearance was with Jimmy Logan and Russell Hunter in *Whisky Galore.* With a smile she recalls, 'I was the only one who didn't need help with the accent, so I knitted a beautiful jumper during rehearsals'.

Cathy-Ann's second album, *Chi Mi'n Geamhradh* (I *see* Winter) eased the clamour that was building up for another album. The advance orders were extremely high. Again she moved a step away from the mainstream in her singing and made use in some of her songs of superb backing from the likes of Savourna Stevenson on harp and Charlie McKerron of Capercaillie on fiddle. In some numbers there is just a whiff of jazz, in others a touch of mainland instrumentalism. Few if any voices have been raised against her approach by those who used to maintain such songs should be sung unaccompanied. The first track, incidentally, which carries the title's name, was written by Calum and Rory Macdonald of Runrig. Once again, both home and overseas critics were warm and generous in their praise, Doug Spencer from Australia's *24 Hours* magazine hailing her as 'the finest Gaelic singer he had ever heard'. Certainly after the release of *Chi Mi'n Geamhradh* her television and radio work increased considerably.

Cathy-Ann's third album largely owes its existence to the film that was made for BBC Television some years ago on the life of the 19th century Skye song-writer, the legendary Mairi Mhor.

Mairi Mhor, 'Big Mary' in English, never wrote a song until she was over 50 and a widow. She was accused of some minor theft, some say wrongly, and sentenced not only to imprisonment for 40 days, but also to banishment from her Island of Skye. Not a happy prospect for someone with five children. The writing of songs became the outlet for her to express the emotions rising within her: songs of anger, songs of longing for her native isle, songs expressing fury against a system which could inflict such cruelty. But also she would write songs expressing the beauty of Skye, the happiness of her childhood and occasionally, humour. Mairi Mhor did eventually return to Skye in the 1880s as Bard of the Land League:

For the children of our people
Driven over the seas will come back again
And the thieving lairds and landlords
Will be driven out, as they were.
The sheep and the deer will be cleared
And the glens be fertile again.

Catherine-Ann MacPhee Sings Mairi Mhor is quite a short CD but there is an extra emotion in the way she sings it.

Recently, Cathy-Ann has taken to teaching the singing of Gaelic songs to the children of three schools on South Uist where she now lives with her husband and two children. Her wide interests include a love of Country and Western music; her unfilled ambition is to learn the pipes.

CHAPTER 10

Strathspey and Reel Societies

A genuine peasant melody of our land is a musical example
of perfected art. I consider it quite as much of a
masterpiece – in miniature – as a Bach fugue or Mozart sonata is
a masterpiece in the larger forms.

Introduction to Contemporary Music – Bela Bartok (1881-1945)

FIDDLERS LIKE TO PLAY TOGETHER. There is safety in numbers and
in a group the not-so-sweet sounding fiddler can make a full contribution. I have no wish to fall out with my fiddle playing friends,
but I have to say, unless a fiddler is a very good fiddler, I would
rather listen to him or her playing in a group where that particularly exciting Scottish sound that is fiddlers in number will stir
whatever it is that flows through my veins. It is that sound, I
believe, that brings people to rallies.

One of the first references to fiddle playing in a group is in the
1549 'Complaynt of Scotland' where admittedly, the strings were
well outnumbered by pipes. Visitors to Crathes Castle can see the
beautiful painted ceiling dated 1599 which depicts musicians playing the fiddle, clavichord, bass viol, lute, flute, harp and cittern.
The cittern was a form of guitar, and those who get a bit uppity
about what is and what is not a traditional instrument might care
to reflect on the long pedigree of some of the instruments that find
favour with folk groups today, if not with certain Strathspey and
Reel Societies.

The main get-together of fiddlers today is of course in what we
commonly call Strathspey and Reel Societies. Some fifty of these
cover the country from north to south and east to west. The
Northern Isles of course, where the fiddle on the wall is almost as
common as a mirror, have active groups. Orkney has its Mainland
and West Mainland Societies as well as a number of less formal
groups. Shetland has its Shetland Fiddlers' Society and on the island
of Yell, the Cullivoe Fiddlers. Youth is well catered for with Young
Heritage, forever associated with the late Tom Anderson, High
Strings, and North, East and West Fiddlers. The Lounge Bar in

The Painted Ceiling of Muses at Crathes Castle

Lerwick, one feels, almost qualifies as a society in its own right. It is not possible to comment on all societies here, but by using a broad brush let us try to get the feel of what is happening throughout the country.

Most societies and fiddle groups will generally meet once a week for practice. Their concerts and appearances in national venues, town, kirk and village halls will range from one to perhaps four outings a month and will be concerned with raising money for charity or just giving pleasure to others. The very large societies who have difficulty in finding stages large enough to accommodate their full membership will limit their full-scale turn-outs to two or three a year and split into smaller groups to meet local needs. Societies have different standards ranging from 'welcome all irrespective of ability' to 'let's see you in action first'. Accordions will fit in with some, others believe anything not drawing horse hair across a high tech cat intestine cannot be termed an instrument.

The average society man or woman is an enthusiast, believing in some modest way they are keeping the culture of their land alive. And this is a true aspiration. Many societies mean much diverse music is being played, and the movement of musicians prompted by attendance at rallies results in an immense circulation of music. It is quite fascinating to see how a particular tune is latched on to after being 'discovered' by one society. Within a few months it is being played throughout the country before finding its billet in the archives. And attendance at rallies makes one aware of different local philosophies and emphasis. Anyone who has heard or played with Inverness Fiddlers for example, and noted their love of bagpipe music, will be aware of how far their programme differs from that of many lowland societies.

But there are two questions worth posing to the memberships of these fiddle organisations. First, are they too conservative (with a very small 'c')? Has everything got to be played from top to bottom without variation? Fiddle playing is on the up and up right now in Scotland. Regretfully, in some quarters there is excessive interest in speed and perhaps a loss of feel for the Scottish idiom and this must be held at bay. But one feels the boat could be pushed out a bit more at times, that some music could be more adventurously orchestrated.

The next question is, are all our Scottish composers being recognised? Some truly excellent music has been composed in recent years. One need think no further than Jim Ferguson of Edinburgh's, 'Skye Jigs', Sandy Ingram of the Angus Society's 'Airlie Lass' and 'Lady Elizabeth's Air', Alex Lawson of Dunfermline's 'Rachael House Suite' and John Mason of the Scottish Fiddle Orchestra's 'Lament for Rev. Archie Beaton'. Somehow or other these new compositions have to be brought to the wider listening public. For too long radio and television have treated this great music movement of ours as being of limited appeal forgetting the extent to which such music is in the blood. And let us be honest, for too long societies have done too little to promote their wares. The name Strathspey and Reel Society is surely today too restrictive. And surely societies should not be afraid to venture into the works of people whose music will disappear if not kept alive. Who better than Strathspey and Reel Societies to include the music of Sir John Clerk, the Earl of Kelly, Oswald, McGibbon, Campbell and so on in their programmes? Should we forget how continental composers have expressed our country in musical terms? The best remembered ones such as Mendelssohn's 'Fingal's Cave' or 'Scotch Symphony' or Bizet's opera the 'Fair Maid of Perth' may be a bit much for most societies. But there are other pieces like Beethoven's 'Ecossaises' or Tchaikovsky's Scots ballad 'Edward' that would make useful items for ringing the changes. The main thing is to avoid the rut that will see audiences and players drop off.

Well, how are our societies faring? Let us look at some of them and the people who take them forward to see what is happening at the local level.

Edinburgh Highland Strathspey and Reel Society

Edinburgh claims the title of the oldest society. But then, music has long been vibrant in our capital city. In the early 1700s Alan Ramsay kept his pen well occupied commenting on the music and dance scene. Even the Music Club existing at that time warranted a special reference in rhyme

While vocal tubes and consort strings engage
To speak the dialect of the Golden Age,
Then you whose symphony of souls proclaim
Your kin to heaven, add to your country's fame,
And show that musick may have so good fate
In Albion's glens, as Umbria's green retreat:
And with Corelli's soft Italian song
Mix Cowdon Knows, and Winter Nights are long.

Concerts in Edinburgh were well recorded before Ramsay's excursions into verse. We know that music teachers were commonplace and a Music Club met regularly in a tavern. While the violin pieces of contemporary composers like Corelli were especially prominent in music circles, the dance assemblies which shot into prominence around 1720 must have ensured that Scottish music was not far off centre stage. And there is one music society we must not forget. The society that gave Edinburgh its regular Gentlemen's Concerts would put its citizens in its debt with the building of the beautiful St. Celia's Hall, today the repository of a harpsichord collection. But let us come more up-to-date.

The legal fraternity always being well represented amongst its members, it is no surprise the Edinburgh Highland Reel and Strathspey Society has a well recorded past. The Society sprang to life on the 26th March 1881 following a meeting of gentlemen 'desirous of forming an Association for the practice and promotion of Scottish National Music, more especially Reel and Strathspey playing in the old Highland fashion on the violin'. From that acorn a mighty tree has grown.

The Society's early life was based around practices in the hall of the Highland and Agricultural Society of Scotland. An early member was J. Stewart Robertson of Edradnyte, compiler of the Athole Collection of Strathspeys and Reels. Hard practice brought financial as well as musical rewards. A concert held in 1884 produced a surplus of eight pounds and twelve shillings, a very sizeable amount of money in these days. By the early 1900s its playing and non-playing membership exceeded 300. With this encouragement the Society went on to make its mark in the Music Hall in George Street before entering the portals of the Usher Hall where it has been seen and enjoyed by many thousands over the past hundred years.

In the hundred odd years of its existence, the Edinburgh Society has only had seven leaders. The continuity of its conductors is even more remarkable. The father and son sequence, Archibald and Ian Menzies, wielded the baton for 50 years while James Calder, always a figure of authority in the Usher Hall, exceeded 40 years as conductor. Today, the Society's conductor is James Ferguson, a beautiful solo player and well known for his appearances with Isobel Meiras, our queen of the clarsach.

Playing in the capital city means the Society makes its mark at many events. It also has a history of its membership breaking down into small groups to provide entertainment at local venues. The Society has a number of well received broadcasts and recordings to its credit. Perhaps even more to its credit is the assistance with music and advice it has given over the years to some twenty-plus societies and groups as they have been formed. Strictly a string orchestra, the piano did not make its entry until 1949. The Society requires those who wish to join it to pass a test of competency in the playing of its music.

Glasgow Caledonian Strathspey and Reel Society

The Glasgow Caley, to use the name it is known affectionately by, has a long and honourable history and has meant something special to a large number of people. This was brought home to me when I listened to the late Archie Findlater being interviewed by Robbie Shepherd in 'The Reel Blend' a few years ago. Archie Findlater, who as a youngster had met Scott Skinner and who was known as the 'Duke of Fife' in fiddle circles throughout Scotland because of his fondness for the tune, played with the society for an amazing 67 years, becoming president and ultimately a worthy honorary president. Not surprisingly for someone whose life was devoted to the Society, he met his wife Charlotte when she came along to play and she notched up 30 years toiling with her bow in the Caley.

The Glasgow Caley Band's roots go back to 1888 when an Orcadian by the name of David Work talked some friends into holding a weekly practice in the bar parlour of the Red Lion in West Nile Street. Growth seems to have been steady although the Society did not have a pianist until 1912, reliance until then being placed on 'cellos and drum. And drum meant side drum only, a bass drum being considered a pipe or dance band item. Tom Sinclair Rae, whose first fiddle lasted his lifetime (he had rescued it from the top of a midden where it had been discarded), took over as conductor in 1921. He became a Glasgow legend, conducting into the 1950s. In the Society's early days, many of the fiddlers could not read music and tunes had to be played over and over again until memorised. A little book was issued to each member which indicated the number given to a set and the titles of its tunes. At a concert, no music was allowed on stage. The conductor indicated the number of the next set and the players, if necessary, referred to their notebook for the tune titles. One wonders how such a system would be welcomed today.

The Glasgow Caley Band seems to have relied quite a bit on competitions to raise the quality of its playing. A silver cup was provided for internal competition in 1934. Proving such a worthwhile approach, the passing years have seen the competition considerably extended, awards going for quartet performances as well as individual classes. Another competition always to be associated with Glasgow of course is the 'Golden Fiddle Award'. In 1976, the then conductor, James Moir, was approached by the Daily Record who wished to sponsor a competition to find the best fiddler in Scotland. It was a competition that captured the public's imagination and culminated in nearly every society in the country being represented somewhere in the senior, junior, or group classes. Elimination competitions were held throughout Scotland with the final event being held in the Kelvin Hall. On that final night, James Moir conducted a massed orchestra of 250 musicians. The old '78' that resulted from that performance is worth listening to today. The effort that was being made by all concerned to make the occasion something special can be felt.

A somewhat different award made by Glasgow is also worth reporting. All the players who served during the war were given Life Membership of the Society and a financial gift as an acknowledgement of what they had done for their country.

One loses track of all the major halls the society has played in, in and around Glasgow: the City Hall, Govan Town Hall, Christian Institute, Lyric Theatre, Motherwell Civic Centre, Kelvin Hall, the Scottish Exhibition Centre: the list appears endless. The society has played the length and breadth of Canada a few times and covered a good bit of Britain. It received world-wide television coverage when it played from the 1986 Commonwealth Games in Edinburgh with Sir Yehudi Menuhin. Many members of the Royal family have attended its concerts. 1979 was a special year for the society. Conductor James Moir was awarded the MBE for his efforts to foster and maintain public interest in Scottish traditional music while the society was presented with the City of Glasgow's 'Loving Cup' which is awarded to persons or associations bringing honour and distinction to the city. The late Ron Gonella once referred to 'the good folk' of the Glasgow Caledonian Strathspey and Reel Society. Today under the perfection-seeking baton of Kenneth McLean, the Glasgow Caley Band maintains that reputation.

The Inverness Fiddlers

To sit on the stage of Eden Court Theatre, Inverness as the curtain rises on a Fiddlers' Rally is indeed a splendid experience. One's first feeling is that by mistake one has landed in an opera house such as La Scala in Milan. Then the eyes take in the design and decor that show the contemporary imposed on the established. In a curious way Eden Court shares and reflects the character of the Inverness Fiddlers who regularly fill this theatre of 800 capacity at their annual rally when well over a 100 musicians take the stage. The Inverness Fiddlers manage to integrate the old and the new. While many of the members have strong musical roots in the area, the Inverness Fiddlers Society was only formed in 1977. It progressed rapidly and today has a playing strength of 50. With a strong bias towards pipe music, it likes to see the pointed notes stressed in 6/8 marches and jigs, and is unmistakably Highland. And while paying due respect to the triumvirate of Gow, Marshall and Skinner the players enjoy contemporary compositions and the music of Scandinavia, a product of the bonds they established with Danish and Swedish groups after playing at a festival in Denmark in 1990. Especially important to the group is its involvement with Phil Cunningham in the presentation of his Highlands and Islands Suite. This new and exciting composition was premiered at the Royal Concert Hall in Glasgow in January 1997 and featured in addition to the Inverness Fiddlers, the Scottish Chamber Orchestra, the Phoenix Choir, Aly Bain, Karen Matheson, the piping MacDonald Brothers from Glenuig and the harp group Sileas. One of the Suite's outstanding arrangements was the dramatic integration of the pipes with the orchestra. The Suite was later performed at Eden Court as part of the Highland Festival in June 1997. At that time Aly Bain was unable to play because of a broken shoulder and his place was taken by local player Duncan Chisholm, formerly of Wolfestone, to great popular acclaim.

The Inverness Fiddlers are particularly well travelled. Besides their regular trips to Scandinavia, they have performed in the Inverness twin towns of Augsbury in Bavaria and La Baule in Brittany. 1996 saw the Fiddlers in action in Cape Breton. To date they have recorded three cassettes and one compact disc.

The Inverness Fiddlers are very much part of the local scene playing at civic events and for charities. Their ties with Balnain House, the traditional music centre opened in 1993, are particularly close. The Fiddlers supply lunchtime music at Balnain House during the summer months and special occasions like the National Mod. Under the Balnain label has been re-published the prestigious 1884 Athole Collection and the Balnain Collection, a book of music by modern composers, is in the pipeline. Many members of the Society serve as 'Friends of Balnain House' and this leads on to Eric Allan, the Fiddlers' secretary, who serves as a director of Balnain.

Eric Allan is one of that rare breed that surface from time to time in the music world. He is widely known as a composer. He has two books to his credit, *Highland Gathering* and *Together* and the entries 'St. Gilbert's Hornpipe' and slow air 'Glen na Muice' in the 'Nineties Collection'. The title music of Grampian TV's 'Ceol na Fidhle' series came from his pen. He writes many of the Fiddlers' arrangements, including the occasional three part harmony setting of classic slow airs. To raise funds for Balnain, Eric offers a 'Tune for £50' service, an offer taken up by those wishing a birthday or wedding gift with a flavour of the unusual. He also offers what he calls a 'slow jam', a once a month music session for the musically rusty who want to get back on stream by playing at a modest pace. Up to 20 may turn up at these sessions. As one might expect from someone who plays guitar and piano as well as fiddle, all instruments are welcomed.

To many musicians of course outwith the Inverness area, Eric Allan is identified as the editor of 'The Fiddlers Calendar'. There has been much talk for years about the need for a communication that would let people know what is happening in the Strathspey and Reel world. Eric and his wife Helen (who is also treasurer of the Inverness Society) have done something about it. There are about 50 major Strathspey and Reel organisations in Scotland, all with the intention, one sometime thinks, of making sure their rallies are scheduled to clash with other attractive events. The calendar, together with other items of news and general information, offers exciting possibilities to all of us who are interested in what is going on. It is to be hoped all societies will help mould the future of this worthwhile venture.

Elgin Strathspey and Reel Society

Many whose life revolves around their local music group get great enjoyment from going to fiddlers' rallies where they renew old acquaintanceships and keep up to date with what is happening in the music field. One of the most popular rallies is that of the Elgin Strathspey and Reel Society. The standard of playing is good, and the crack makes the longish journey worthwhile. Some say the proximity of the Speyside distilleries has something to do with it and comment on the 'apres rally' ceilidh. But the Elgin Society is one that has had its ups and downs and has ended up all the stronger for that.

To explore the Society's roots, one must travel back to the 1920s, to the village of Lhanbryde. There, the local headmaster, one Colonel Reid, was an enthusiastic fiddler and the leader of an entertainment group known as the 'Dominie's Concert Party'. Squeezed, sometimes ten to the car, the party played all over Moray and Banff. It was personnel who played in the concert party or were associated with it in some way who, in 1936, decided it was time for Elgin to have its own Strathspey and Reel Society. The inaugural meeting was held in the back shop of the double bass player and later Lord Provost's music shop. The Aberdeen Society which then had ten years' experience under its belt, gave advice and assistance. The subscription was set at two shillings and sixpence. The editor of the local newspaper sought assurance the new Society was not going to interfere with any other groups operating in the town. The first concert raised funds for the Elgin YWCA.

War disrupts life and the Society closed down for the duration. 1947 saw history repeat itself as some hardies returned to George Smith's back shop to breathe life back into the old Society. The concert party tradition was still in the blood. One member played the saw. Another provided monologues, others sang. In the August of 1948 the society, now numbering 20, broadcast for the BBC from the Gordon Arms in Elgin. But at a time when people were leaving the district and Scottish music was losing its head of steam, the orchestra found the going difficult and again went into abeyance in 1950.

Some things however cannot be battened down. Twenty years later, local man Willie MacPherson who had seen service with the Scottish National Orchestra returned home. Gathering together another seven enthusiasts and the forty pounds that lay in the bank from earlier days, the Elgin Society sprang to life playing within a week for the local branch of An Comunn Gaidhealach. From there on, the Society's story is one of success. Taking entry into the competition field seriously, after an apprenticeship period, the Elgin society in 1972 won the orchestral competitions in both Banchory and Kirriemuir. Two years later, to mark the 750th anniversary of Elgin cathedral the first rally was held. The Society's annual rally, which has continued since then and is held in the 760 capacity Elgin Town hall is inevitably a sell-out. As a thoughtful touch, the junior section is given a spot at the rally and a guest artiste of standing is normally present. The Daily Record 'Golden Fiddle' competitions inaugurated by that national paper in 1976 were an irresistible magnet. Within a five year period, Elgin had two first and two second placings in the group competitions while musical director Brian Brown in 1974 achieved the accolade of Golden Fiddle Champion. In another three years, the society would win both the 'Golden Fiddle' and 'Mod' sevens, and sweep the boards at Kirriemuir, Banchory, Aberdeen and at their own festival in Elgin.

The Elgin Society has seen a bit of the world. The town is 'twinned' with Landshutt in Bavaria and has twice given concerts in that region of Germany. In 1990, the Society made for the rather unusual venues of Jersey and Sark.

As befits the county of Morayshire, the world of the fermtouns is not neglected and the Society's president, Eric Simpson, is a regular singer of bothy ballads at concerts. Eric, who has figured in the prize lists at competitions held in Kirriemuir, Keith and Strichen, reckons 'Bogie's Bonnie Belle' is the classic bothy ballad with 'McGinty's Meal and Ale' not so far behind.

In their distinctive blue tops the 30 playing members of the Society have a heavy schedule in the North-east. If there is a worry, it is the absence of young people joining the Society. The fiddle tradition in the area is particularly strong, and there are good school groups like the Fochaber Fiddlers and the Speyside Fiddlers at Aberlour. But a lack of jobs in the area means many drift away from one of the most attractive parts of Scotland. Hopefully, they do not leave their fiddles behind.

Fife Strathspey and Reel Society

The Counties of Angus, Perth and Fife have long been famous for the profusion and quality of their country dance bands. Shand, the Camerons, Ian Powrie, Adam Rennie, the Hawthorne Band, Robb Gordon, Bobby Crowe, Bert Shorthouse: the list is apparently endless. Their prominence has to a degree masked the activity of their more sedate colleagues in the Strathspey and Reel field. Yet, in this field the three counties have much worthy of acknowledgement.

The Fife Strathspey and Reel Society does not celebrate its quarter century until the millenium, yet has achieved considerable status. Its energetic patron in the Earl of Elgin and the holding of its annual rally in the Carnegie Hall, Dunfermline gives it a certain something. Its first conductor was Bruce Turnbull who, a few years after getting the show on the road, moved north where he would form the Garioch Fiddlers, a busy and much respected group in the northeast. And so it was that Jim Laing returning from a holiday received the news that, in his absence, he had been appointed conductor, a position he was to hold for just under 15 years.

It has to be admitted Jim Laing's musical career is somewhat different from that of most societies' conductors. It started normally enough with piano lessons, but his father's work movement to Wales saw the young James take to singing and he performed as an urchin in Carmen, the Welsh National Opera's first post war production. As Skiffle hit the scene and became his love, Jim took

An early photograph of the Banchory Strathspey and Reel Society

to the banjo and, the family moving again, this time to Kent, it was not long before he was in a group performing both in regular venues (ten shillings for an eight pm to five am Friday/Saturday stint) and an assortment of London West End and Soho coffee bars. As skiffle died its death, the trombone became his instrument and he somehow managed to combine evening classes at Trinity College of Music with playing in a dance band. One suspects there might have been some relief evident when he received a work promotion which brought him back to Scotland. As a second instrument he had long practised on his father's fiddle and on his return north, he joined, first, a string group, before responding to an advertisement advising the formation of the Fife Society. As already noted, his promotion to conductor was abrupt, but in charge he took a particular interest in arrangements, studied harmony and orchestration academically (courtesy of the Open University), and then gave up conducting to concentrate on fiddle playing. Always a believer in the busy life, Jim has been a stalwart of the Scottish Fiddle Orchestra since its inception in 1980 and more recently has made a full contribution to the concert and musical journey life of the music group Quern. He is also proud of taking part in Scotland's smallest fiddlers' rally. A certain 'rural' in a fit of enthusiasm advertised a fiddlers' rally without, apparantly, enlisting the support of local groups. Jim was one of the three fiddlers who turned up. A mini concert was managed, and, as a bonus, Jim was invited to judge the baking. One of the others was luckier. He won a pair of tights in the raffle!

The Fife Society has a number of special events to its credit. They have played three times in Germany in the Glenrothes twin town of Boblingen, near Stuttgart. They have broadcast on BBC Scotland and appeared on television with Harry Secombe when his 'Highway' programme visited St. Andrews. Amongst their charity efforts, their annual concert in the Brunton Hall in Musselburgh for the Royal Blind Asylum warrants a special mention.

While the Fife Society regards Kirkcaldy as its home and heavily draws its membership from the Kingdom, their along-the-road neighbour, Dunfermline Caledonian Strathspey and Reel Society, has a scattered membership drawing players from Kinross to Grangemouth to Livingston and all points between. This is not to suggest animosity since the two societies are on the best of terms. Conducted by Ron Smith, Dunfermline is one of the younger societies and has two composers in Alex Lawson and Helen Lockhart in its ranks.

Conductor Ron Smith's relationship with his fiddle has had its tenuous moments. His, father being self-taught on the fiddle, decided that Ron should have the best of teachers. He was somewhat displeased (the actual quote was, 'he threw a fit') to discover the expensive lessons were being bypassed as his son sneaked off to learn the cornet. That issue had scarcely resolved itself before Ron took up the pipes, ultimately becoming Pipe Major of the 67th BB Band. But there was to be no escaping from music, and on leaving the Air Force after National Service he took up the career of organ builder. It was a job, he recalls, which meant living away from home and the fiddle only came out of its case at weekends and holidays. But he certainly retained his touch. He joined the Dunfermline Society when it was formed and circumstances dictated shortly thereafter that he should take over the baton. Ron is another example of a musician who has little time for barriers in the music field, happy to be involved in the ceilidh and country dance scene, welcoming all instruments into the society.

Amongst the many fine players in the Dunfermline Society one must mention Elisabeth McLay. Elisabeth hails from New York State and so fell in love with Scottish fiddle music at the Stirling Summer School, she elected to remain in Scotland. This year Elisabeth won the Ron Gonella Trophy for Slow Airs and shared the top honour at the annual Musselburgh festival of accordion and fiddle clubs.

Elisabeth McLay

Stirling Caledonian Strathspey and Reel Society

It is an impressive record. For more than 45 years, the Stirling Strathspey and Reel Society has operated under the baton of a man called Cook. The weel kent face recognised in Scottish music circles that is Bill Cook's has been in charge for 27 years. His father took over in the 1950s. But first a look at Bill Cook's musical career.

A native of Central Scotland, Bill Cook studied fiddle under his father and his teenage years saw him involved with young friends in a country dance band. They cut their teeth on the odd village hop before becoming the regular outfit that played in a church hall in the small town of Sauchie every Friday night. Being an ultra respectable gig it finished before ten o'clock and Bill recalls how the band then made their way as quickly as possible up to the weekly country dance in the Crook of Devon. This was a dance with a bit of a reputation where the big names regularly performed. It was enough for the young Bill just to sit and listen to the likes of Angus Fitchet, Jim Cameron, Bobby McLeod, Jimmy Shand, Alistair Downey and especially his musical hero over many years, Ian Powrie. One night when some of the musicians were having tea, Ian Powrie invited Bill to play with him on stage. Talking with him about this all these years later, one still senses the thrill that accompanied that invitation.

Bill's early intention was to be an architect and such studies followed school. As he donned uniform to undertake National Service, it was not surprising that he was directed into the Royal Engineers. Nor was it all that surprising that the Sappers should identify his musical talents and post him to the orchestra of the Corps. Bill enjoyed his army period so much he stayed in uniform until 1966. The army, of course, offers travel and the orchestra played extensively throughout Europe. But army musicians are required to do more than fill concert halls. The army marches and instruments that can be played on the hoof as it were have to be learned. Bill wryly relates how he started on the cymbals which would be followed in sequence by the drums and the trombone. A better trombone player arriving on the scene, Bill was transferred first to the euphonium and then finally to the majesty of the E flat bass. He seems to have fallen in love with this instrument, his Colonel Bogey solo being much admired. To further his musical abilities, the army allowed Bill to attend classes over a two year period at the Guildhall School of Music in London and there Bill studied the theoretical aspects of music, giving particular attention to harmony.

Bill returned to 'Civvy Street' a family man. During the time he was trying to readjust to civilian life, he resumed his architectural studies and started to play with the local Jim Dawson's Country Dance Band he had played with before army service, making his first broadcast in 1970. Then a lucky card was dealt to him. Clackmannan Education Authority decided to appoint a tutor to oversee the learning of the strings in schools. Bill applied for the job, was successful, and, to coin a phrase, lived there happily ever after.

We now turn to the Stirling Strathspey and Reel Society where Bill's name is so highly regarded. The society had been formed in 1930 by two brothers called Harvey who hailed from the Whins of Milton. The Society grew and prospered and had broadcast pre-war when such a thing for an amateur orchestra was unusual. Bill's father was involved with the Society. He seems to have been an unusually talented man. In addition to playing the fiddle and clarsach, he was a choirmaster and conductor of a local orchestra. In the early 1950s he became the Stirling Society's conductor, and shortly after his death in 1969, his son Bill, still in his twenties, took over the baton. The reputation of the Stirling Society is high and as their ability to fill the 800 seats of the Albert Hall in Stirling shows, they are well liked by the local population. They do not include accordions, although Bill claims that is more to do with the problems of accommodating non-string instruments on stage at concerts, than antagonism against that instrument. As one who frequently sits by the side of box players with country dance bands and has more than his share of appearances on 'Take The Floor' to his credit, this makes sense. The Stirling Society numbers 60 with a sizeable junior section also on stage at concerts. Unusually, and perhaps uniquely, the Society always include something from the classics in their annual concert. Vivaldi's 'Four Seasons', 'The Queen of Sheba', and Strauss Waltzes, have all made appearances.

In 1983, Bill Cook was appointed leader of the Scottish Fiddle Orchestra. Of his experiences with that orchestra, one that was full of enjoyment was playing in the air from Glasgow to New York to an audience of travel agents when a new flight was being inaugurated. A less enjoyable experience was a sea journey between Orkney mainland and one of the smaller islands when the players found themselves hanging on by their fingertips as a frightening sea played havoc with their stomachs. Given the advice that singing prevents sea-sickness, the musicians tried their best to coax out some notes, whether to the beat of the engines or the sea is not known.

Bill Cook, of course, is known to many because of his compositions. He traces his beginnings as a composer to when he found it
difficult to find suitable material for his classes at school. His published tutor, *Guide to Scottish Fiddling* which came out in 1986 has
stood the test of time and is a standard shop item. In all he reckons
to have written around 200 tunes. The week following the Dunblane tragedy, the Stirling Society were scheduled to play their
Annual Concert in the Albert Hall. With some members of the
orchestra coming from Dunblane, it was felt that some acknowledgement was appropriate. In two days, 'Lament for Dunblane' was
written and played (naturally without applause) prior to the com-
mencement of the concert.

Much use of his lively and catchy compositions are made by
his pupils and junior members of the Stirling Society as they perform on a solo basis. He recognises a change in public taste, at
least in Central Scotland, over the past 20 years. The more serious
and difficult pieces have been superseded by lighter tunes with
catchy melodies. He cites 'Shiftin' Bobbins' as an example and
gives great credit to the country dance band composers like Jim
Johnstone and the late Andrew Rankine. Audiences, he considers,
have developed a taste for hornpipes. But he also says, 'there's no
substitute for the old played well'.

In conversations about fiddlers, the names of Ian Powrie and the
late Willie Hunter of Shetland keep creeping in. Bill is a frequent
soloist at concerts where Hunter's 'Leaving Lerwick Harbour' is one
of his favourite pieces. He plays it, one feels, as a very personal tribute to an old friend. Although basically a fairly laid-back character,
he is well known for the promptness with which he responds to
appeals for help. A nice story on which to end is the quiet way he
has helped the Perth Society to raise funds for their coming Canadian tour. A talented artist, Bill has painted an 'orchestra of insects',
all beavering away with their instruments. This painting he has
given to the Perth Society to copy and sell.

Shetland Fiddlers' Society

This society has its origins in an unusual event.

The need to emigrate has long been a feature of Scottish life, and
the country's extremities, the Northern and Hebridean islands, have

probably suffered from this more than the mainland. The islanders though, in the main, emigrated to take up work in the old colonies, (weren't ninety per cent of the Hudson Bay Company's factors supposed to be such people?) where their basic culture could be reasonably maintained. In 1959, a group of exiles in Wellington, New Zealand, conceived the idea of making a return visit to Shetland in one large party. It was one of those ideas which capture imaginations. The home Shetlanders planned ever increasing entertainment to welcome the returning exiles. On hearing of what was being planned, more exiles, from all over the world, decided to join the inward flow. The upshot was the occasion, now christened the Hamefaring, became the biggest cultural event ever held in the islands, surpassing in scale even the famous annual Up-Helly-Aa fire festival.

It is not surprising that Shetland music played such a central part in the proceedings. Let me quote from the Fiddlers' Society profile sheet:

'Shetland has a musical tradition stretching back to the time of Norse influence, founded on the timeless necessity for melody and rhythm to lead and accompany the act of dance. The tradition, subject to musical influences from all over Europe, produced a

Shetland Fiddlers Society

style of playing and distinctive tunes unique to the islands, and although by 1960 other forms of music-making and dance had taken root in Shetland, it was still very much alive.'

The comment about the relationship between music and dance will strike a chord with many people.

The key figure in arranging the musical side of things for the Hamefaring was, of course, Tom Anderson, who at that time led a band of fiddlers associated with the Shetland Folk Society. Anderson now organised 'Forty Fiddlers' to play at Hamefaring concerts. The response from both exiles and home Shetlanders to their playing was so tremendous that a movement grew to ensure the 'Forty Fiddlers' would become a permanent feature on the social scene. And so the Shetland Fiddlers' Society came into being with Tom Anderson as its first leader, and incidentally, a youth called Aly Bain as its youngest founder member. Within a matter of weeks, they were playing before the Queen and the Duke of Edinburgh when they visited the islands. A recent note from the Society indicates a playing membership with an age range from 11 to 81.

The Shetland Fiddlers' Society has gone from strength to strength over the years. The society has played over much of Scotland and England, been seen on television and recorded splendid cassettes. From a distance one senses a special relationship between the society and fiddlers from Cape Breton, exemplified in that fine tune 'Cape Breton's Welcome to the Shetland Fiddlers' by the late and much lamented Willie Hunter, one of the many, outstanding musicians who made their mark while a member of the society. In 1994, the Shetland Fiddlers' Society received the prestigious Europa Prize for Folk Art Awards. It was perhaps appropriate the award should be handed over in Germany, because at one time fiddles were a regular import into Shetland from that country.

Tom Anderson, now no longer with us, has a secure place in music's Hall of Fame. His crowning achievement must be the keeping of Shetland's music alive in a recognisable form, making it strong enough to withstand the pressures coming at it from Scottish music (many Shetlanders regard bagpipes as foreign instruments) and radio (at one time because of better reception from American than UK stations, jazz was a major influence). For his services to Shetland music he was awarded the MBE in 1977. He was a man

who 'got around' always keen to teach his Shetland style of fiddling both in Shetland and on the mainland, in places like Stirling
University's Heritage of Scotland Summer School which he supported for many years. Tom Anderson was a notable collector of
old Shetland tunes, but it will probably be his compositions which
will carry his name forward in the coming years. He was extremely prolific and many of his compositions are yet to arrive on music
shop shelves.

In her book, *Life in Shetland*, Ursula Venables gives a flash-
back to the wedding customs of the 1830s.

'There was a procession headed by the fiddler, then the gunner
and his firelock. They walked six miles to a house near the manse,
where clothes were dried out, a good dram of whisky was taken,
and the fiddler jigged away at the "Brides March". Then the company entered the Manse, the Minister performed the ceremony,
another glass was offered for the road home and the fiddler played
the "Brides Return". Once home, they dined and drank and
danced, and the fiddler saw the night away with his reels.'

Before closing this journey round our fiddle societies, there is one
memorable event to be recorded, an event which has entered the
annals of traditional Scottish music. Its television title was
"Yehudi Menuhin's Welcome to Blair Castle" and the fiddlers for
the occasion were drawn from the membership of the Banchory
and Angus Societies. The conductor that night was the late Sandy
Milne of Banchory, a character if ever there was one, as will now
be shown.

Sandy Milne came from near Tarland in Deeside. He was fiddle mad as a youngster and would follow Scott Skinner round his
various engagements. Skinner after his concerts would sell, not
CD's like to-day's players, but rather high-priced photographs of
himself. The young Milne was determined to have one and not
having sufficient funds, had no qualms about vigorously negotiat-
ing a more acceptable price. Unfortunately he made the mistake of
later giving the photograph to a girl friend who in turn thought so
highly of it she would not return it to him when their friendship
came to an end. Her behaviour he considered unbecoming and it
rankled with him for years after. Snaring rabbits at six pence a
time helped the youngster to eventually buy his own fiddle. Sadly,
it had a short life. Returning home one snowy night after playing

at a dance, with his fiddle carefully wrapped in a green baize bag, he had to cross the Tarland Burn. Cautiously he threw the instrument across the burn on to a snow covered bank. As he took a running jump to clear the burn, the fiddle started to slide down the bank and into the water. He landed right on top of it.

Sandy Milne came home from the First World War, where he was wounded three times, to settle in Banchory. Ever active with the fiddle he would in due course found the Banchory Strathspey and Reel Society. While appearing as guest conductor at a rally in Oban one year his exhortations, delivered in his own style, to the fiddlers to "use their crannies" (their little fingers) brought him to the notice of the BBC and he was invited to conduct an orchestra brought together one night in a certain television series which featured choirs, orchestras and the like. On arrival however, the conductor to be was horrified to discover that, unlike himself, the fiddlers had not memorised the tunes and intended playing from music. Sandy Milne would have none of this. The place for music stands he stated, "was in the Clyde". A forceful discussion followed the upshot being that those who could play from memory were placed in the front row. Those who could not sat behind them, reading from music pinned on the back of the jackets of those in front. One can just imagine the problems faced by the cameramen.

Obviously good camera, Sandy Milne was the conductor chosen when the BBC started to make preparations for its programme, "Yehudi Menuhin's Welcome to Blair Castle". Inevitably, one of the world's greatest violinists and Sandy Milne found the odd musical item to argue about. A study of correspondence, however, shows the existence of a bond of respect and indeed affection. A favourite story is that of the two men discovering a common interest in bee-keeping with Sandy Milne's ire rising as not all his words of advice were accepted. "Listen" he is reported to have said to the great man, "maybe, just maybe, you can tell me something aboot fiddling, but ye canna tell me onything aboot bees".

The performance of the combined Banchory and Angus Societies on that night at Blair Castle in 1979 has gone down in history. It was put on at a time when interest in fiddle playing was stirring. The flood of letters both to the BBC and to Sandy Milne provided the proof that the night had indeed been something special. Those of us who saw the programme on television, will never forget it. Those who were present and saw Yehidi Menuhin practise his yoga during the rehearsal have another tale to tell.

The national culture of music of every people rests on a healthy relationship between folk music and composed music. Only the music which has sprung from the ancient musical traditions of a people can reach the masses of that people.

Zoltan Kodaly (1882 – 1967)

CHAPTER 11

Jim Reid

Wi' hand on hainch, and upward e'e,
He crooned his gamut, one, two, three,
Then in an arioso key,
The wee apollo,
Set off wi' allegretto glee
His giga solo.

The Jolly Beggars - **Robert Burns**

SOME CHILDREN, THEY SAY, are born with a silver spoon in their mouth. In Jim Reid's case it seems to have been a 'moothie'. His attachment to the instrument is complete. He has played it as far back as he can remember and it still figures in his encounters with song today.

If one were to be washed up on a desert island with a folk singer, then Jim would be the choice companion of many. Eminently practical and good with his hands, he is an uncomplicated character, unassuming yet direct. What you see is what you get. The voice that speaks is the voice that sings, unmistakably east coast and within the 'road and miles of Dundee'.

Although he confesses to always singing, it was not something that dominated his early life. Sport was of much more interest to him. In the Boys Brigade he learned the pipes, sang in the odd 'get-together' and concert during his period of National Service but musically leaned towards jazz. Special favourites of these early years were Ella Fitzgerald and Nat 'King' Cole. After the army, football and athletics continued to be his main interests. But in due course he accepted an invitation to join a folk group that was being formed in his native city and from there on a new life seemed to open up. Taking a cue from The Weavers who were riding high at this time, the group from the jute city called themselves The Shifters adopting Mary Brooksbank's 'Oh Dear Me, the Mill's Gaen Fest' as their signature tune. The group prospered in the local growing folk club scene, got occasional engagements as support to a big name, and generally enjoyed the fun that goes with four sizeable men and their instruments being squeezed into a mini. The group's material was Clancy Brothers slanted and one suspects it was performed with some vigour. Jim Reid confesses to being happy at that time going round the clubs and improving his guitar playing. When, because of work movements The Shifters broke up, it was with little enthusiasm he accepted an invitation to join The Taysiders. Yet the years he spent with The Taysiders were important in his development. While still on Clancy Brothers

Jim Reid

type material, he was exploring his own ability to write songs. When Bob Dylan in the age of protest wrote 'Times They Are a-Changin' Jim lifted pen to write his own song, 'Who says, Times are a-Changin'?' But perhaps more important for his long term reputation he, to use his own words, started to dabble with poetry. Left alone in a room full of books one day, he had discovered the works of Violet Jacob and like so many others who felt they had discovered hidden treasure when coming across her poetry for the first time, he consumed it avidly. And for that discovery Jim Reid and the folk who like folk music would, as will he seen, benefit.

Life with The Taysiders gave Jim the experience of appearing on television, but greater prominence was coming his way. A change in employment meant a move to Arbroath. A 'pie and a pint' was a favoured lunch and in the course of seeking a pub that comfortably met his needs, he chanced upon the Foundry Bar. There he found a place frequented by town, farm and fisher folk with happy crack. And as a bonus the bar had music nights when the place bounced. Here Jim Reid was in his element. Mouth organ, guitar and song, not to mention the occasional appearance of pipes were his offerings and he was soon to the fore. The collection of musicians who gathered in the Foundry Bar decided that the forthcoming TMSA Festival at Kinross was worthy of their support, and in due course almost 20 of them took to the stage to be greeted with enthusiasm. The Foundry Bar Band as it came to be called had arrived and would prosper. It won many trophies at festivals, and regularly played at ceilidhs and major events. While the name of Jim Reid would always be associated with the Foundry Bar Band, it is perhaps not always recognised the effect it had on him as a singer. The band was made up of a number of robust characters who were not prepared to put down their instruments and listen while he exercised his vocal chords. They were there to play, and play they would. Jim was now forced to bridge the gap between the folk scene and the Scottish dance scene. On his own in the past he had been concentrating on the old ballads like 'Laird of Drum' and 'Lang Johnnie More'. Additionally, he had become friendly with the great travelling family, the Stewarts of Blair, and this had given him a greater insight into the depth of Scottish song so that he was singing many songs to old, and to him, previously unknown tunes. Now he had to sing songs the band was playing, 'Tramps and Hawkers' for waltzes, 'Bonnie Lass o' Fyvie' for the Gay Gordons. In fact he claims to have been the only person to have sung on Robbie Shepherd's 'Take the Floor' when the band did an outside broadcast. Exciting as it was to link up with the Foundry Bar Band, it did seem to involve him in something akin to a culture shock.

Jim had joined the TMSA some years earlier and had served as a committee member and as chairman. His main achievement, though, was the setting up and organising of the festival the TMSA wanted to see off the ground at Keith. The continuing success of this festival, which he regularly attends, is a testimony to his efforts.

It is only when one sits cracking to Jim Reid that there is a full appreciation of his very considerable input into the wider Scottish scene. Following a meeting at the Edinburgh Folk Festival with Billy Kay whose Odessy programmes were making their mark, he collaborated with Kay on radio programmes about the Dundee jute workers, Angus country life, Bothy Ballads and Violet Jacob as well as two television programmes concerned with dialect. With Joy Hendry he appeared in Arbroath and Montrose paying tribute to Violet Jacob. It is now 25 years since, to considerable acclaim, he first sang Jacob's 'Rohallion' on a Grampian Television show. His setting of her 'Wild Geese' pulls at the heart of more than Angus folk, while his latest CD features Jacob's 'Hallowe'en'. 'But no more recordings of Violet Jacob', he says. 'I don't want to spoil what I have done'. His compositions, poems, tunes and songs number around 60. A lot of people would like to see a major publication from him. One song that he has made his own is the very nostalgic 'Scattered'. This was given to him by a well known Dundee piper, Pipe Major Angus McLeod. The words, very much from the heart, were written by the Pipe Major's grandmother who saw almost all of her ten children scattered from their native County of Angus to all the ends of the earth. The poem was published in the Peoples Journal in 1890. Pipe Major Mcleod set it to the music of Lord Lovat's Lament.

In 1988 Jim Reid crossed the Atlantic. Belle Stewart had been due to take part in a traditional song event in America but had to withdraw through illness. Jim Reid went in her stead and for a week in Pine Trees Camp in Massachusetts, he took a song workshop every morning, a bagpipe session every afternoon and made his contribution as required every night. He fondly remembers writing a 'thank you' verse for the students to the tune of Margaret's Waltz which was appropriated, copied and sung back to him as he was leaving. His respect for Belle Stewart is obvious and one senses his regret that Alec Stewart died before hearing the pipe tune 'The Stewarts of Blair' he had written for the family. Amongst other journeys he remembers with affection are his appearance with the Foundry Bar Band at the Tonder festival in Denmark when nearly 5,000 listened to the band and his annual visits to Ireland, now stretching to 7, with An Teallach.

Casting an eye over the folk scene he comments, 'When we started there were great singers and good musicians. Today there are brilliant musicians but few great singers.' He expresses the fear that songs may be tampered with to allow the instrumentalist greater licence. He accepts tradition involves evolution. If bongo drums come in, so be it. But the expressed fear is that influences from other lands may disperse what is essentially Scottish. It is difficult to envisage Jim Reid changing his own style in any way. With a video and two CDs in the pipeline, we can look forward to hearing that honest but rich voice for some time yet.

CHAPTER 12

The McCalmans

Wi' quaffing and laughing
They ranted an' they sang,
Wi' jumping an' thumping,
The vera girdle rang.

"The Jolly Beggars" – **Robert Burns**

TO MANY, THE MCCALMANS represent continuity in the Scottish
folk scene. And it has to be said, with a career spanning over 30
years which includes, besides world-wide concerts, the regular
issues of albums, annual Highland tours and appearances at the
Edinburgh Festival Fringe on top of innumerable radio and television appearances, their name is well known to many who never
cross the portals of folk clubs or read *Living Tradition.*

The media have always been important to the McCalmans. To
the media Ian McCalman owes his enthusiasm for folk music. The
singing of Jimmy Macgregor and Robin Hall on the legendary current affairs programme 'To-Night' captured his imagination. He
loved listening to the records of Pete Seeger, the Kingston Trio and
particularly The Weavers. The Corries and Paddy Bell figure
strongly in his recollections. With his guitar playing brothers he
would experiment with arrangements for the tunes published
weekly in Norman Buchan's weekly article in *The Scotsman* and
destined to be published later in Buchan's *Hundred and One
Scottish Songs.*

There is a suggestion of Providence or fate in the story of how
The McCalmans came into being. Ian's career intention on leaving
school was to be an architect and having presented himself at the
appropriate college of learning was directed on his first day to a
particular studio to undertake a simple exercise. Happily engaged
with 'T' and set square he started to whistle a little known tune.
Two nearby first year students picked up the tune. Within minutes
he discovered Derek Moffat and Hamish Bayne were as addicted
to folk music as he was and within two days they decided to form

a folk group. The original intention, Ian recalls, was that they would practice for a year before seeking gigs.

What happens to best laid plans is well known. Having a drink together one night they asked the hostelry owner if they could sing a song. He agreed and following the customers' enthusiasm for them they were asked to come back the next week for a two hour performance. They happily accepted, ignoring the fact their immediate repertoire did not exceed two songs. The first fee of thirty shillings seemed like a fortune and from then on with gigs coming quickly, architecture took a back seat. With a slight blush in the cheek, Ian admits they started off billing themselves as Ian, Derek and Hamish. After a few weeks this was changed to The Callants. Becoming more image conscious and accepting the fact Ian was the only one with a telephone, they matured to the Ian McCalum Folk Group. Their material was Scottish, drawn from the traditional and harmonised to suit their voices. The backing to their songs came from guitars and mandolin, with whistle and concertina added as appropriate. Two years later they made use of their college holiday to make an English tour. Engagement offers were now literally pouring in and the papers were acknowledging both their efforts to provide harmonies which had impact, and their insatiable appetite for new songs.

The McCalmans

Aware that the architectural qualification was on the verge of disappearing, the trio gave serious thought to giving priority to their studies. Fate though had another idea. Ben Lyon, the BBC producer, contacted them with the offer of radio engagements. In these days, such an offer was something only the faint-hearted could turn down. The trio set off to broadcast both from studios and village halls throughout the country. At the end of the series discussions about their careers again dominated their lives. They decided that recording a 'demo' record following a recording audition would be a fitting finale before relegating music to a hobby. But the recording studio sensed their potential and persuaded them, if much persuasion was needed, to make an album, a rather uncommon thing at the time. The album was duly made, and the group now received the attention of the London press. Other recording companies approached them. Thoughts of careers apart from music now disappeared completely. 1972 saw the group with their own radio programme which was followed by a series on BBC Television. A later series on Grampian Television brought its share of problems. Much of their material had to be pre-recorded and one of the wettest summers on record meant the trio standing in damp and wind swept locations faking vitality and bonhommie as they mimed their songs.

By now The McCalmans were no strangers in Europe. In 1966 they had busked in Denmark for 3 weeks and developing a love affair with that country have returned almost every year. Shortly afterwards, Holland and Germany were added to their tour venues. Most groups have a tale or two to tell about life on the road, especially about accommodation. Ian's favourite story though, is a beauty.

In their early days they were booked to give a concert in Brittany, it being explained to them they would be taken to their 'digs' after their performance. It was a successful gig and into the wee small hours when their French guide escorted them to the front door of a house, giving them the key with the quite insistent instruction they had to be out of the house and the key returned by a certain time the next morning. The house, they soon discovered, possessed no light and was empty of all furnishings except for mattresses in one room. In an exhausted state they fell asleep to be wakened in daylight by a tremendous bang which made the building vibrate. They rushed to the window to come almost face to face with a crane wielding a huge ball and chain. With the real-isation the building was being knocked down, they grabbed their belongings, the French workmen staring in disbelief as three tou-sled musicians scurried out of the house like rabbits from a bur-row being chased by a weasel.

In the early seventies The McCalmans were approached by Combined Services Entertainment to undertake a tour round over-seas service establishments. It was a considerable experience, play-ing not only in the more civilised stations of Cyprus and Malta but desert and jungle outposts in Oman and Belize. Returning to civil-ian life, further tours would see The McCalmans make their mark in Australia and North America. They were one of the few groups to appear in East Germany before the wall came down.

While two Australian tours had gone without a hitch, a third ran into agency difficulties as it was being organised and the group decided to cancel it. They could not however cancel an arranged stopover concert in Hong Kong as the tickets had already been sold. To help defray the hefty expenses of what was in effect now becom-ing a one concert tour, Ian filled a large suitcase with cassettes, hop-ing a charitable and understanding customs officer (perhaps a Scot) would be modest in his tax demands. He was not quite prepared for the Chinese official's attitude. In response to the inevitable, 'Any-thing to declare?' Ian opened his suitcase showing around 200 McCalman cassettes. The inscrutable official commented, 'I meant, have you anything of value to declare?' Ruminating on the flight and concert, Ian continues, 'The meal that night must have been the most expensive carry-out ever.'

It was in Canada in 1981 Hamish confessed that after 19 years he was attracted to a more settled existence and he wanted to give the other two a year in which to find a replacement. The search for a replacement was not hurried but in due course Nick Keir came in as a worthy successor to Hamish. The group's line-up con-tinuity over a 30-odd year period is something of which they can be proud. It was a handover devoid of any acrimony and the friendship continues to this day. Hamish of course has developed a business making his Holmwood concertinas which have achieved world-wide sales.

The early material of The McCalmans was essentially Scottish. While they can never be considered other than a Scottish group, their material over the years has changed. While obviously it is a generalisation, one can chart their material movement from searching for the unused traditional in their earlier days through the setting of poems to music to protest type songs and observations on the contemporary scene. Their poetry sources were varied. They liked and used the works of contemporary poets like Stewart Conn and Pete Morgan but did not shy away from the different 'Lays of a Scottish Cavalier'. They have eschewed the advent of the Celtic swing and adhered to their own style, still seeing themselves as singers rather than instrumentalists. A firm base workload in Europe where their popularity continues to be strong allows them to 'gang their own gait'. Their 1997 appearance at a prestigious event in Kenya, the sales of 21 albums, and their regular radio appearances all show that even after 33 years, The McCalmans are still in business.

CHAPTER 13

Sheena Wellington

And in some hour there comes delight
When thorter's flesh forgets its thrang
In flight that is abune a' flight
And sang that is abume a' sang.

– **William Soutar** (1898-1943)

SHEENA WELLINGTON IS A true daughter of Dundee. Her humour, at times thrawness, pride and 'couthiness' all spell out the place made famous for jute, jam and journalism. This is not to imply parochialism. The city built round the Law has long sent its sons and daughters to the ends of the earth, and they have returned to the city or its environs with greater worldly insights, assurance and added attachment to the place of their birth. Sheena is of that mould.

The young girl grew up in a musical environment at home. In her house everybody sang everything, from ballads to Burns, psalms to street songs. A bonus was a nearby hall where country dances were held and the great bands of the fifties like Jim Cameron's and the Hawthorne could be heard by youngsters content to stand outside and inhale the music during the country dancing hey-day. At school, Sheena sang in the school choir, performed solos at Christmas and other concerts and gradually came to the fore as a singer. She became a Leng Medallist, that much coveted award given in a competition open to all Dundee schools. The song she selected was 'The Winter It Is Past', and her love of Burns has stayed with her. Indeed, it prompted a question she would often ask at school: 'Miss, why am I supposed to speak "proper English" in your class and "proper Scots" when reading poetry and singing because it is Scottish culture?' That confusion may not quite have left her.

It is probably fair to say that the folk revival of the early sixties did not have the same impact in Dundee as it had, say, in Glasgow, because Scots and street songs were still very much to alive amongst the general population. But in keeping with the rest of the country, a folk club opened up in Dundee and Sheena became a regular attender. It took a while, she confesses, before she mustered enough courage to take the stage. Her choice of songs at that time were still the muckle ballads, but Joan Baez and Bob Dillon were impressing her mightily. The age of protest was now creeping in. Songs about Polaris and the Holy Loch abounded to such effect the teenage schoolgirl took off with fervour to squat with others outside the American base. The police were not impressed. One wonders how many watching a most respectable looking Sheena Wellington adjudicating at a song-contest today, know of her dreadful past: arrested in Dunoon and fined five shillings. And one also wonders what was said in the school staffroom?

Not long after leaving school, Sheena joined the WRNS and was posted initially to Lossiemouth, taking the oportunity to sing in various hostelries in that area. Then she became a serviceman's wife and for the next 14 years was to find herself occupying accommodation in many parts of the UK. One senses this was important to her singing life as well as her private life. She talks enthusiastically about singing in the English West Country and, sticking to her own Scots stuff, how well she was received. In this new environment she was cutting her teeth on audiences from different traditions, accustomed to different music. It was experience to stand her in good stead later on.

When Sheena and her husband Malcolm eventually quit service life they settled in St. Andrews where they opened a guest house, satisfying an ambition they had held for some time. As luck would have it, within a few doors was a folk club. From being a regular attender she became first the club's regular singer and then its compere. As family and guest house commitments allowed, she began to go to festivals and the name Sheena Wellington began to take prominence nationally.

Sheena has, sometimes to the chagrin of others, a questioning mind. As local radio became a part of our lives she felt it was not catering for all its listeners' needs. Radio Tay as the nearest station took the brunt of her annoyance. 'Why', she wanted to know, 'is there not a folk music programme?' Not receiving a satisfactory answer she kept writing letters making her point. Her insistence was rewarded. Radio Tay offered her a 6 week trial running her own programme. The trial was to last 8 years. The spin-off for her was considerable. Through the medium of radio she entered thousands of living-rooms, established herself as a prominent figure at least in the East of Scotland, and brought many national figures such as Hamish Moore, Belle Stewart, Dougie MacLean, Jean Redpath and The Corries to her studio to be interviewed. Her meeting with Belle Stewart ripened into friendship. Sheena is unstinting in her praise for Belle's singing, and speaks fondly of her wisdom, hospitality and quick wit.

Sheena's first album *Kerelaw* came out in 1986 and had considerable success. It contains her own composition 'Newport Braes': a particularly fine rendering of 'The Irish Boy' and, capturing the emotion of the time, 'The Last Leviathan'. But one of the high spots in her singing career was now arriving. In 1989 she accepted an invitation from Dougie McLean to accompany him on a coast-to-coast tour of the States. It was a blistering tour involving over 20 flights in 14 days. In a somewhat optimistic gesture, she modestly admits, she packed a hundred of her albums. How wrong can one be? They were all sold out after her first appearance. No less than four times in that fortnight did copies of *Kerelaw* have to be flown out to venues. Before an audience of 3,000 in Los Angeles she established herself as one of Scotland's finest folk ambassadresses. She returned to the States the next year, again with Dougie McLean, while 1991 saw her in the Maritime Provinces of Canada with the Vale of Athol pipe Band. McLean she regards as a complete professional always conscious of the importance of high standards. Of her many memories of these North American tours, there are two she loves to recall where perhaps unwittingly she reveals much about herself. First there is the affluent black executive who after listening to her sing 'My Ain Countrie' remarked she was singing his history as well as her own. The second was the discovery of people in the States who eagerly await the arrival of the Beano and Dandy from relatives in Scotland. She cannot tell you about this with a straight face.

If only considered as a performer, Sheena Wellington's place in the folk song scene in Scotland would be assured. But she has also 'put something back' into the music life that has given her so much pleasure. After serving as secretary of the Traditional Music and Song Association, in 1990 she became its Convenor. From there, she accepted the invitation to serve on the Scottish Arts Council Music Working Group, later serving on its Music Committee for five years. She is a Trustee of the Arts Trust of Scotland, a Fellow of the Society of Antiquaries and an Honorary Life Member of the TMSA. She is known as a doughty campaigner for greater investment in Scottish traditional and folk music and song and a school curriculum where Scottish culture in all its forms is more strongly positioned. Although she retains the words of an abundance of songs quite perfectly, Sheena is capable of forgetting other things. Her answer is to set important things to music. Attending a Burns Supper in Singapore not so long ago, she was asked at short notice to give the 'Address To A Haggis'. This she did, 'Words by Burns, music by Wellington'.

Today, when singing, Sheena Wellington still conveys the impression that she believes in the words of her songs. To put it simply, she sings with sincerity. And it is refreshing to come across someone who, while admitting there is a Scottish kitsch that is best forgotten, will give unstinting praise to the mark that Harry Lauder and Andy Stewart made in the world as Scottish entertainers. She journeys a lot (Ireland seems to be a favourite haunt), thinks her country is more confident than hitherto and has no doubts Scottish culture in all its facets is advancing on a broad front. While not a prolific composer or prominent in the recording world, one feels 'The Women of Dundee' is going to be around for a long, long time. And that, as they say, is where we came in.

CHAPTER 14

Mairi Campbell

For in four frail gut strings I know
All music sleeps for me to wake,
And here before the peat-fire glow
Fine melody I'll make.

"Fiddler" - Robert Service (1874-1958)

To speak with Mairi Campbell is to speak with someone totally immersed in the Scottish scene be it fiddling, singing or dancing. With song-writing now creeping into her repertoire, her talents are indeed formidable.

Yet the Scottish musical scene was not her early world. Although with a full share of Highland blood in her veins, it was the music of the classical masters that dominated the first part of her life. Her first instrument was the viola to be followed later by the piano. Of her three sisters, two played the violin and the other the 'cello. Thus, there was no need to travel far to experience the joys of a string quartet. Mairi entered the Broughton Music Unit in Edinburgh for her last two years at school where again the music she was playing centred around the classical. In fact she confesses her only close contact with Scottish traditional music was on holiday, at the dances on the Island of Lismore. These dances she had loved, responding both to the music and the movement to it. But at this point in time she was thirled to the classics and from Broughton she moved to London to enroll at the Guild Hall School of Music where she would study viola for nearly five years under Lsaba Erdelyi, then violist with the Chilingirian String Quartet. From the Guild Hall, she made the fairly normal step into orchestral life and joined the Kreisler String Orchestra. This, she recalls with a smile, was a most unusual outfit. There was no conductor or musical director and the repertoire and rehearsals were treated as they would be in a string quartet with everyone having an equal say, something which led to long rehearsals but thrilling and competent performances. The orchestra travelled widely. The memory of sympathetic audiences in Russia listening with glisten-

Mairi Campbell

ing eyes to the orchestra playing the music of their land such as Shostakovich's Chamber Symphony has stayed strongly with her. The playing of Bartok in Hungary was a challenge too, but it was in Amsterdam that fear took over. The Kreisler was sharing a concert with a local orchestra and it had been arranged they would combine for the last item. It was Mairi's turn to act as librarian. After the afternoon's rehearsal the members of the Kreisler returned to their hotel. They performed their part of the concert in the evening and left the stage to allow the local orchestra to play. It was while thinking about getting ready for the finale that Mairi discovered she had left the music for concluding the concert in the hotel. She had ten minutes to return to the hotel, lift the music and make it back to the concert hall. She returned to the concert completely breathless and with a pumping heart as the musicians were taking the stage.

But like many an exile before her, London-based life eventually palled and she returned to Edinburgh. Mairi had some vague notion she would like to become more acquainted with Scottish music, and over the next six months took an interest in what was happening around folk clubs and the like. But she was still unsettled, had itchy feet and took off for North America.

After crossing the Atlantic Mairi visited various relatives and travelled around. She remembered that before she had left Edinburgh, Margaret Bennet from the School of Scottish Studies had told her about the fiddle music scene in Cape Breton. In conversation after performing in the Toronto Folk Club one night, she asked if anyone knew of a contact in Cape Breton. The names of Alec and Minnie MacMaster were given to her. She made telephone contact with them and accepted their generous offer to stay at their home for a few days. Little did she appreciate at that time she was entering the house of future world star Natalie MacMaster, niece of the legendary fiddler and highly respected Buddy MacMaster.

There is more than a hint of a 'Road to Damascus' conversion associated with her introduction to Cape Breton music. Its impact was immediate and strong and she knew that in traditional music she had found the something she had been looking for in her life. The playing of strathspeys in particular touched her. She understood what people were saying when they talked about the alliance between the rhythm of the Gaelic language (very widely spoken in Cape Breton until recent years) and the Cape Breton music. She felt what had been lost to Scotland over the years. The vitality of the step-dancing so strongly tied into the music, too, entranced her and she succumbed to the ambience of a place that were it not for the winter weather, one would consider as near to paradise as one can get.

Her meeting with Buddy MacMaster has a certain 'couthiness' attached to it. She had attended a church service where Buddy had played a Lament. Afterwards she was introduced to Buddy as a 'wee Scota lassie who plays the fiddle'. Later on he asked her to play along with him and she quickly perceived that in Cape Breton such requests are accepted as a matter of courtesy, irrespective of one's ability. Temptation came her way to remain in Canada when she was invited to play viola in a string quartet operating from Newfoundland. But by this time she was fired up with the idea of playing Scottish music in Scotland the way it was interpreted in Cape Breton, and, after visiting other parts of Canada, she returned to Edinburgh. But the next year she returned to Cape Breton to study at the Gaelic College at St. Annes. Cape Breton fiddle and step-dancing were her subjects. She has returned to the College since, both to study and to teach.

In 1991 Mairi met her husband-to-be Dave Francis. They flirted around the band scene for a while before deciding to form a duo called The Cast, an arrangement which has stood the test of time. In addition to her instrumental skills, Mairi has a rich voice and puts over a song in a natural way, while Dave, an experienced and imaginative guitarist provides the backing and works on the lyrics. The following year the couple went to the Gaelic College at Teangue in Skye where Alisdair Fraser, the brilliant fiddler now based in the States, was leading a fiddle course. There they also met Alistair's brother, Ian, who had set up Culburnie records and who invited

Mairi and Dave to record an album for his company. Their first album, *The Winnowing*, had much success and was followed by *Colours of Lichen*. In their second album, Dave's skill with words is brought into play to merge beautifully with Mairi's tune in 'The Piper and the Maker'. It is a particularly imaginative piece of work, composed with thought and well worthy of attention.

Mairi's viola is heard to good effect in these albums. Indeed one wishes more use was made of the rich tones of a viola in the traditional and folk scene. But her fiddle has been more than busy over these past years. A meeting with Freeland Barbour brought about an invitation to join The Occasionals where she is a regular and has played with them in Denmark and at the redoubtable Accordion and Fiddle Festival annual dance in Shetland. Mairi admits to a love of playing for dancing where the concentration has to be on timing and rhythm. Completely at home and assured when singing on stage, she confesses her fiddle pleasure is at its highest when playing for dancing be it country dancing or step dancing. The dancing in the ceilidh world is not ignored. Presently Mairi and Dave are trying out a new ceilidh sound where three fiddles, guitar and double bass combine to give a good strong rhythm and lift. One of the benefits of course of having such an experienced dancer as Mairi in the line-up is that the dancers can expect timing that is spot on, something many ceilidh bands have yet to achieve. Having served a long apprenticeship herself, one senses she feels some resentment when musical standards on stage are not what they should be.

Although the Scots field is her main love, Mairi has not completely forsaken the classics and freelances from time to time with the BBC Symphony Orchestra, the Scottish National Orchestra and the Scottish Chamber Orchestra. She was particulary pleased to be asked to play with the SNO when Natalie MacMaster gave her 1997 concert in the Usher Hall in Edinburgh. Sometimes, when playing the classics, she forgets where she is as when recently in the middle of a Beethoven Symphony a fellow player had to ask her to stop tapping her foot. One of her most interesting comments is that playing Scottish traditional music has helped her understand the classics better. She is able to see the music in simpler terms, to take it, as it were, off its pedestal. In playing the classics she sees the emphasis being placed on melody and the production of tone. In traditional music, especially for dancing, it is the timing, phrasing and rhythm that require the concentration.

Tone is of course important. It has to be strong but not necessarily so refined as demanded in the classical field. Mairi emphasises the point that the serious composers have been, and indeed still are, greatly influenced by the traditional music of their country. She is convinced that if classical players would seek an involvement in traditional music, they would gain an added feel for the tune and its required 'lift' and, as a consequence, the classics would become more attractive to a wider audience.

Mairi has naturally been involved with her husband Dave's musical story-telling projects like 'The Lang Reel' and 'A Winter's Night' and with Hamish Moore and Ryan MacNeil in their promotion of Cape Breton music. With a young family, much of Mairi's time is presently spent on teaching rather than touring. One wonders how many musicians are capable of tutoring across so many fields. Classical violin and viola, folk fiddle, chamber music, voice and dancing all figure on her schedule. But one bit of travel she made in 1997 warrants a mention. The Cast were one of the few Scottish performers from Scotland to be invited to the Celtic Colours International Festival, the first such festival to be held on the Nova Scotia island of Cape Breton.

CHAPTER 15

Fiona Ritchie
– the Thistle and Shamrock

*In the evening the company danced as usual. We performed,
with much activity, a dance which, I suppose, the emigration
from Skye has occasioned. They call it 'America'.*

Journal of a Tour of the Hebrides – James Boswell, 2 October
1773

ONE OF THE LESSER KNOWN benefits of the 1707 Treaty of Union
was that Scotland, at long last, was allowed to trade directly with
the English Colonies in North America. In the wake of trade came
settlement and the early eighteenth century saw a few hundred
Highlanders, mainly from Inverness, Kintyre and Islay, ensconced
in the area we now know as North Carolina. Following the
Jacobite uprising of '45, oppression and the Clearances saw this
exodus to North Carolina increase, another 15,000 arriving by the
mid 1770s. Amongst these later arrivals were Flora Macdonald
and her husband Allan. Within six months of their arrival, Allan
and Flora were to find themselves in leading roles as Loyalists as
friction grew between the settlers and the American government of
George the Third.

It is doubtful if Fiona Ritchie, then a 19 year old psychology student at Stirling University, thought overmuch about the detail of
Scottish settlements in North Carolina as she settled down in the
University campus in Charlotte on a six month's student exchange.
She was startled by signs proclaiming Ceud Mille Failte, ill prepared
for Highland games of the size of the Grandfather Mountain gathering and with some disbelief discovered a college where the Alma
Mater was sung in Gaelic. But to someone who liked to sing, and
whose taste in music centred around the Battlefield Band, Breton
harp and Planxty it was an easy environment in which to settle.
Particularly, she enjoyed the 'back porch' old time music sessions
she attended with friends, but felt let down by local radio stations
who ignored the existing wealth of regional music and concentrat-

Fiona Ritchie

ed on what was happening in the pop music charts. However, she was now hooked on North Carolina and after returning to this country and completing her degree course, 1981 saw her back in Charlotte, North Carolina.

In the intervening period a new radio station, one of the public radio stations being set up at that time, had become operational. And it was a station not reluctant to provide both local news and indigenous regional music. Over the ether came Appalachian dulcimer, Cajun fiddle, blues and jazz music. Fiona landed a job with the station, not as a broadcaster, but as the person responsible for fund raising and the station's development. One suspects, though, her charms must have been at work as shortly after taking up her appointment, she was invited, or perhaps it was allowed, to present a weekly programme playing the records that had accompanied her back to the States. Returning home for Christmas, she made contact with Scottish, Irish and English recording companies, once again used her powers of persuasion, and arranged to be supplied with new releases for her programme. So we see the beginning of her work to let America (and bits of Canada) know what is happening over here.

Public radio continued to grow in the States and by 1983 Fiona's programme, now the well known 'Thistle and Shamrock' had hooked up to the other stations and achieved national coverage. In 1990, with over 330 stations linking up to her hour-long programme of Celtic music, Fiona made the decision to form her own production company which she felt would allow her to tighten the link musically between Scotland and the States. Today she operates from her offices in both Charlotte and Edinburgh.

It is only when one starts to look in depth at what Fiona Ritchie has been doing these past years that the fullness of her work comes to light. Three thousand letters a month come to her from

Americans wanting more information about Scotland, many from people who have heard Scottish music for the first time because of her programmes. And these programmes are not solely music or music with interviews. There is frequently what can be described as an educational or cultural input. Many of her programmes are based around themes: life styles, working life, trades or perhaps a particular aspect of music such as Celtic guitar. She issues a news sheet for visitors coming to Scotland and wanting information of a 'What's On' nature and has donated much of her working material to St. Andrew's Presbyterian College in North Carolina, making it the largest archive of Scottish music in the States. She is much in demand as a compere at events such as those organised at Wolf Trap, the National Park for Performing Arts, near Washington. Recently in Chicago, she narrated the city's tribute to Chicago's legendary Chief of Police, Captain Francis O'Neil who died in 1936. It was O'Neil who over the years would interview immigrants as they arrived from all over Ireland, writing down for posterity the music and songs they were bringing with them from their homeland. The nine volumes he compiled were to be returned to Ireland when that country became aware of how much of its cultural heritage had been allowed to slip away unrecorded. Fiona's professionalism has been widely recognised as the awards hanging on her office walls testify.

The popularity of her programmes in the States have prompted many of the now 350 radio stations that take her programme to undertake their own investigations into and promotions of Scottish and local links. Two examples will suffice to show the benefit to Scotland of Fiona's programmes. The public radio station in Fairbanks, Alaska, set out to show the Scottish affiliations of the native Athabascan tribe who had been introduced to Scottish music, song and dance by the early fur traders of the Hudson Bay company, the majority of whom were recruited from Orkney and the Outer Hebrides. Her programme in Fairbanks, incidentally, is sponsored by the local Red Hackle Pipe Band. Some dancing was involved and as the Athabascans sorted out their sets it was noticed one set was a lady short. Although nonplussed, Fiona stepped into the breach. The steps of the dance, she remembers, were akin to a travelling step with a shuffle. Her experience registered with me. I remember the surprise I felt when I encountered a brilliant Micmac fiddler in Nova Scotia. It prompts the question: how often do we think of our heritage being enjoyed by other peoples in far away places?

At the other end of the continent Fiona enjoyed a night with her linked station near Baton Rouge in Louisiana when the focus was on cross Celtic-Cajun culture. Cajuns of course stem from the French population of what was at one time called Acadia, now known as the Maritime part of Canada. Unable to convince the British Government of their complete loyalty to the crown, the Royal Navy in 1755, shipped some 18,000 of them down the coast to other colonies from where they dispersed inland. Their story has been immortalised in Longfellow's poem, 'Evangeline'. Fiona well remembers the broadcast. It was going out live yet she was expected to dance every time the music started. It was, she recalls, her most breathless broadcast ever.

In recent years Fiona has been heard on radio in the UK. Her accent, still essentially Scottish after many years in the States, has been heard both on Radio Scotland and BBC 2. Her overview of the folk scene takes in the drift to more formality, the concert-based approach. The issue of more independent labels she sees as a welcome development. She is impressed by the number of young people wanting to play traditional music while recognising their wish to experiment with what for a long time has been considered sacrosanct. She has a hunch an explosion of Scottish song may be round the corner. Now spending much more time in Scotland, she has too much restless talent, one feels, to be content only with what she has achieved so far.

CHAPTER 16

The Accordion and Fiddle Club Movement

*For you've chided me in weakness and you've
  cheered me in defeat:
You've been an anodyne in hours of pain;
And when the slugging jolts of life have jarred me
  off my feet,
You've ragged me back into the ring again.*

"Accordion" - Robert Service (1874-1958)

THE DIRECTORY OF THE National Association of Accordion and Fiddle Clubs lists the names and addresses of some 73 secretaries. A look at the club venues shows the tentacles of this active organisation stretch from Shetland in the north into the County of Northumberland in the south. The Outer Isles are not neglected although the eyebrows raise a trifle at an address in Ireland and one in Vancouver.

Our story starts back in 1965. Max Houlison, the eminent accordionist who hails from Dumfries, was concerned about the demise of concert parties which for years had given young players the opportunity of developing their musicianship in front of a live audience. He had available premises in the 'Hole in the Wa' in Dumfries and formed an Accordion and Fiddle Club to meet the need. The idea caught on and prospered. Pioneers in Gretna and Milngavie followed Max Houlison's lead and before long it was evident that a movement was underway. The club evenings followed a pattern that has changed little over the years. Players of all ages are given the chance to perform (normally a couple of selections), there is a performance by a guest artiste or band and the evening ends with a 'stramash' – all players on the floor. These clubs, then, allow the amateur to see the professional close up. And, as a point of interest, it was never laid down in the tablets by Max Houlison that all the music played in his club had to be Scottish.

As audiences started to build up and people showed the desire to travel further away to see particular artistes, the need for a national organisation became obvious. Additionally, there was a growing enthusiasm for an event which would draw a wide range of musicians together and allow them to display their talents in competition. In 1971, the National Association of Accordion and Fiddle Clubs came into being. Its first Chairman was the well known band leader Mickie Ainsworth. Shortly afterwards, the first Musselburgh Festival was announced. History was in the making.

1998 sees take place the Twenty-Fourth Annual Accordion and Fiddle Championships. As usual they take place in the Brunton Halls in Musselburgh. During the first event the manager of the halls was one Jim Johnstone. Today, that same Jim Johnstone is Chairman of the Association. The Musselburgh championships represent a vast piece of organisation offering competitors of all ages entry into a wide range of classes. To win an award at Musselburgh is indeed to obtain a worthwhile accolade.

But the National Association perhaps presents a more relaxed and congenial face at its annual general meeting at Perth. Amidst all the socialising, the tradition has grown of honouring the greats of the Scottish music scene at a special luncheon. To begin with, a large portrait photograph was the vehicle used and recipients included Jimmy Shand, Angus Fitchet, Bobby MacLeod, Ian Powrie, Andy Stewart and Jimmy Blue. More recently a Caithness Glass bowl has been awarded to Jim Macleod and Max Houlison, while, in a most thoughtful gesture, a special scroll has gone to the Accordion and Fiddle Club in Shetland to acknowledge the unique contribution that place has made to our Scottish culture. A slight digression to comment on the Shetland Festival would not be inappropriate here.

Now in its tenth year, the festival organised by Shetland Accordion and Fiddle Club is entering the realm of legend. In short, it is a four day bonanza with musicians arriving 'frae a' the 'airts', although that is not Shetland speak. While based around the Isleburgh Community Centre in Lerwick, sessions and dances are organised throughout the islands. Some musicians may have four ferry journeys to make in one day before their heads touch the pillow. And smooth seas are not guaranteed. The festival reaches its peak at a grand dance at the Clickimin Centre when twelve bands take the stage for half hour sessions to make sure there is no respite for the 800 dancers. A video has been made of the event. It is well worth buying or borrowing.

Progress, of course, depends on people, and the National Association has been blessed with many who have given years of solid service. A look at the background and contribution of Charlie Todd, the present secretary, provides a good example of what some people both get from and give to our world of music. Charlie comes from the Lanarkshire village of Thankerton. His parents were accordion players so not unexpectedly he took to the box at an early age. His parents, though, were wise enough to send him to lessons at the age of 13 from the much respected Jean Brown of Wishaw, where, he wryly remembers, the emphasis was on the classics, traditional music still being regarded as *infra dig*. By the time he was 20, though, he had made the decision to take the playing of Scottish music seriously and he became involved with the Biggar and Lesmahagow Clubs. Indeed, he has served as treasurer at Lesmahagow for 15 years, which, some may think, serves him right for being an accountant. In his early twenties he also fulfilled an earlier ambition by joining Lanark and District Pipe Band to learn the side drum. Pipe band activities dovetailed nicely with Accordion Club work, the former starting in May and continuing through to September while the latter started in September and finished in April. The rest of the year, he claims, was his own.

Charlie's extra qualification as a drummer has proved to be useful in helping him to see the world. A friendship established with top piper Peter Wood of the Biggar British Legion Pipe Band, who is also a very good accordionist, opened doors for him. Before long the two of them joined with Keith Dickson to play for Edinburgh University's New Scotland Country Dance Society in Norway and later in the year in Poland (still then behind the Iron Curtain). A further trip to the Netherlands followed shortly with another band.

The Island of Sicily holds many street parades at the time of Epiphany, and there is a connection there between the nativity scene and the bagpipes. Courtesy of the Sicilian Tourist Board Charlie went to Sicily wielding his accordion and with a troup of dancers to provide music when the pipers were having their break. It was a happy arrangement which lasted for three years. 1992 saw Charlie take off to play at the Caledonian Ball in Nairobi in Kenya. This has become almost an annual event for him. The one year he could not make it, the compensation was to play at a British Trade Fair in Tokyo. On one occasion Peter Wood, now playing with Ian McPhail's Band, was unable to travel and Charlie stepped into the breach thus including Hong Kong and Taiwan Caledonian Balls amongst his campaign medals, which now also include Abu Dhabi.

In due course Charlie formed his own outfit, electing to call it the Cameronian Ceilidh Band, which is particularly active in the Edinburgh-Glasgow area. An enthusiast for calling dances, he enjoys the more relaxed atmosphere at ceilidh dances as compared with playing for country dances. However, like many brought up in the world of set dancing, he is concerned about the lack of attention to timing and detail shown by some ceilidh bands.

However, if travels, playing with the Cameronian Ceilidh Band and being secretary of the National Association were not enough, Charlie has found time to add another string to his bow. Not long ago he took over the editorship of the Association's journal, *Box and Fiddle*.

The *Box and Fiddle* started life as a news-sheet to let members know what was happening around the clubs. Now it has blossomed into a monthly 'glossy' of 24 pages. Although Club news makes up the bulk of its contents, there are reports on new releases and music as well as who is going to appear where. Charlie has introduced speciality articles like 'Composer's Corner'. Circulation extends outwith Scotland to the Falkland Isles, New Zealand, Canada and the States. Charlie sees himself as putting something back into an interest which has given him so much pleasure.

Always interested in the export of Scottish culture, Charlie had a go at listing the destinations of Scottish musicians who left our shores to play at St. Andrew's Night functions in November 1997. He would not claim his list is exhaustive; it isn't; the writer can add one or two names. But this is what he came up with: Jersey, Guernsey, The Hague, Berlin, Warsaw, Moscow, Sofia, Geneva, Cairo, Casablanca, Kuwait, Bahrain, Oman, Jordan, Kampala, Nairobi, Singapore, Kuala Lumpur, Hong Kong, Taiwan, Bangkok, Seoul, Jakarta, Delhi, Dhaka, Caracas, Bogota, Mexico City, Rio de Janeiro, Sao Paolo and Montevideo.

Forres Accordion and Fiddle Club is one of those bastions of music that are so liberally sprinkled over the North of Scotland.

A welcoming club, it is not one to be missed when in the area. The Forres Club opened its doors on Burns Night 1978 when Graeme Mitchell, who had just won the Scottish championship, and his band honoured the occasion. Such was the enthusiasm in these early days that membership had to be restricted to the hall's capacity of 275. Even today, with such clubs now in a settled state, membership is not far short of 200.

Inevitably, those in with the bricks have stories to tell. Bobby MacLeod played at the club the year after it opened while a snowstorm was raging. He was seen safely into his hotel around half past eleven at night and the following morning a club member telephoned The Mishnish, Bobby's hotel in Tobermory, to advise of the snowstorm. To his surprise, the robust Macleod answered the 'phone. 'I was once snowbound in Forres before,' he explained, 'and didn't want a repeat. I knew if I could get to Inverness, I could follow the bread van down to Oban and jump the first ferry.' Stories of Macleod's quotes of course abound. 'There's only one way to play a pipe march,' he would say, 'and that's right.'

The Forres Club has entertained many of our top box and fiddle players, but by common consent, one of the club's most magical evenings was in 1981 when the Hamefarers from Shetland made Forres their venue on one of their few mainland visits. The members got their money's worth that night; Willie Hunter on fiddle, Jim Halcrow on accordion, Ronnie Cooper played piano, Ronnie Hunter on bass guitar and Douglas Johnston on drums. Another great club favourite was, and still is, Ian Powrie. It is claimed Powrie made his mind up to return to Scotland from Australia for good after being moved by the music of two youngsters playing in the Forres Club in June 1983.

A real club stalwart is Andy Ross who has served as president, secretary and regularly as compere. Andy, of course, is known to a very wide audience in the north through his programmes on Moray Firth Radio. His request programmes and *Andy's Ceilidh*, have loyal followings and have brought the personalities of such as Bobby Brown of Canada's Scottish Accent and the characters that make up the Wallochmor Ceilidh Band into the home. Many a musician too, like Bobby Coghill, Ian Powrie and singer Alasdair Gillies has appeared on his *Moray Firth People*.

A shepherd's son, Andy knows the value of radio to those in less populated places. He remembers the great dance bands of the mid-fifties to mid-sixties and how, in that time of musical explosion, the village halls had to compete to get the best bands. In these days leading bands had a following of dancers that ensured financial success.

Asked about today's scene, Andy rates 'Margaret's Waltz' as the most popular tune and Jimmy Shand and Addie Harper as the most requested bands. Speaking as a fiddle and box man he gives top marks to veteran Bill Black and young player Steven Carary. But he does go on to lament the shortage of qualified accordion teachers in the north. Speaking of the annual Shetland Accordion and Fiddle Festival (cleverly arranged during the Tattie Holidays in October), he is ecstatic. The arranging of six scattered concerts a night round the islands is, of course, a prodigious task. But it is the thought of that final night in the Clickimin when around 800 dancers turn up to dance to perhaps a dozen bands each being given a half hour slot, that makes the mind boggle. 'See Naples and die', they say. I'd rather see the Shetland Festival.

CHAPTER 17

ALP - the Scots Music Group

Shall we sae sour and sulky sit,
Wi' neither sense, nor mirth, nor wit,
Nor ever rise to shake a fit
To the Reel o' Tullochgorum.

"Tullochgorum" - John Skinner (1721-1807)

THERE IS A PART OF EDINBURGH that bounces with music most nights of the week. Not, it is added, a part of the city known for public houses and cafes nor even its concert halls, but a part that houses nondescript school buildings. And it is from these buildings that emanates the sound of fiddles and accordions, whistles and bodhrans, and a range of other instruments, not to mention songs and the animated discourse of dancers. For this is ALP at work, the Music Group of the Adult Learning Project, to give it its full title. It houses in excess of 400 people striving to become more actively involved in the Scottish musical scene. The spin-off, in terms of individual enrichment and the strengthening of the country's musical culture, is inevitably less obvious.

There was a considerable gestation period to the setting up of ALP's 'Scots Music Group'. In 1988 the Adult Learning Project as part of what was then Lothian Regional Council's Community Education Department, launched a new programme of classes and events under the title, 'Scotland and its People'. At that time history, politics, land issues, Gaelic and so on, provided the material. Two years later, the decision was taken to include music in the programme.

Any new venture depends greatly on the person given the responsibility of getting the show on the road. In this instance, the right person was at hand. Stan Reeves was not only working as a Development Officer with the Project but was actively involved in the music scene as a member of the well known Robert Fish Band. He quickly made use of his contacts in the business.

The growth of the Scots Music Group is not to be looked at

simply as the prodigious expansion of a series of night classes. The Project has another agenda. An ideology is involved.

The consultative group, set up in 1989 to look at the position of our traditional music in the community, came up with findings that many will recognise. They were perhaps city findings more than country findings but, of course, none the less relevant for that. The group identified a 'tartanry' which trivialised our music and bemoaned the fact that the various component parts of our culture, dancing, piping, the Strathspey and Reel societies, Fiddle and Accordion clubs, folk clubs and so on seemed to exist in their own small worlds. In other words, music was seen as some kind of hobby rather than being a central component to our national culture and contemporary life. The group felt that there was not an opportunity for people, and especially young people to learn and enjoy Scottish music in a social environment. A new approach was needed.

To meet these findings the Project decided it was essential to hold the various learning opportunities on the same night in the same venue. These 'clusters of classes' would integrate further musically and socially, by means of 'pub sessions' and local concerts. Not all classes would teach a single instrument; some would be open to people who just wanted to play with others irrespective of what instrument they played single instrument classes would learn the same tunes to ease the transition to playing with others. And, perhaps contentiously, teaching (learning would be a more accurate description) would encourage playing by ear or memory. Having established what it wanted to do, the sleeves were rolled up.

In 1990, 60 people enrolled for classes in fiddle, whistle, guitar and song. The following year 120 enrolled for ten various over-subscribed classes. The next year's increase strained the structure to such an extent (the number of music students now exceeding the main project) a special Scots Music Group had to be formed from students and staff to run alongside the ALP Association, taking joint decisions about policy, fees, promoting the music through performances and liaising with other organisations. Promotion through sessions, concerts and ceilidhs brought in more students as names from the professional music scene appeared as tutors. Specialist workshops to augment classes appeared on the scene. In 1996, 200 fiddlers would attend a workshop at a new 'National Fiddle Festival' run by ALP, while other students supported workshops in whistle, flute and pipe and Cape Breton and Scots dance.

Today over 400 people from all walks of life are attending these Music Group classes. Operating in a democratic way with students being given full opportunity not only to express their views but to become involved in the running of the Music Group, there is no sign of the pace slackening. This is not to suggest everything in the garden is rosy, or that all issues have been resolved. Two areas are worthy of enlargement here.

The majority of tutors are drawn from the professional and semi-professional music ranks. The strength of this is that they have a level of expertise which commands respect, and are willing to pass on all the little short cuts that other music teachers might not admit existed. But, just as good footballers do not necessarily make the best managers, neither do professional musicians necessarily make the best tutors. There is a shortage of skilled tutors in the traditional music field, and ALP has had, as Stan Reeves puts it, 'to create them'. And when they are trained, they are liable to be enticed away with offers of work elsewhere. The problem has been well recognised and tutor recruitment and training arrangements extended considerably. But one feels there is still work to be done in this field, and this leads on to an issue that, while of importance to ALP, may have national importance as well. What is the best way to have the average person in the street learn to play an instrument socially as easily and quickly as possible?

ALP firmly flies the flag of playing by ear. It claims tradition and results are on its side. This approach contains many options. Should music be issued after learning a piece for reinforcement purposes or not at all? Should prepared cassettes be issued in advance of classes with a view to speeding up class progress, or issued later for recall practice? Does a tutor start at the Three Blind Mice level and slowly progress to the hard stuff, or should he or she select initially something that is not easy but which has the 'I'd love to be able to play that' aura? In other words, there is a need for more research into how best to tackle the learning and playing by ear approach, making use of modern advances in training technology. The success of ALP is going to encourage similar development in other parts of the country. It is, as already suggested, a national issue. Don't let us finish up in a situation where the wheel is being invented many times over. Once the best approach to learning and playing by ear has been identified, it will be easier to set out a teaching structure for music tutors to become learning facilitators.

There are other areas where ALP has done or is doing worthwhile work. Concerts and workshops such as 'Fiddle 97' in the Assembly Rooms, Edinburgh, which allow the amateur to see those at the top of the tree, such as Alisdair Fraser, in action at close range have tremendous motivational spin-off. Workshops catering for the often neglected refinements such as 'dance calling' and 'hand percussion' add to overall standards. The regular exchanges with places outwith Scotland such as Cape Breton and the Celtic folk of Brittany and Ireland enriches all involved. The bands that come together in the Music Group before going their own way, such as the six piece Da Hooley who took part in Hong Kong New Year celebrations, encourage others to take their musical development a stage further. And perhaps most importantly of all, we note the work the Music Group is doing with young people. Contact with primary and secondary schools has resulted in children becoming aware of their musical heritage who otherwise might never have known about it. This year's 'Youth Gaitherin' brought together 100 children for four days in a starter group, two fiddle groups and two mixed instrument groups. Future plans for those young people are ambitious.

CHAPTER 18

The Greentrax Label

It helps a lot, with throat or lip
In life's contentious coil
To make a pretty partnership
Of melody and toil.

"The Music Makers" – **Robert Service** (1874-1958)

TODAY'S LIFE DEMANDS READY access to music. The miles pass more quickly with a cassette playing in the car. The sitting room in the house is somewhat naked without a CD player. Joggers and school-kids seem half-clad without their Walkman. The shopping mall is a desolate place without its background sounds. In an incredibly short time the Scottish music production scene, responding to both musi-cal and technical change, has gone through an amazing metamor-phosis. Forty years ago Scottish music lovers stacked their records of Jimmy Shand and Jim Cameron or whatever dance band took their fancy on a fireside table. Thirty plus years ago the avant garde bought cassettes of Andy Stewart and the Alexander Brothers. Today the cassette, which on its arrival opened up opportunities for recording previously not available, faces a limited future as the com-pact disc carries the scene. The range of artistes offering recorded entertainment from the traditional to the innovative has multiplied many times.

Some people thrive on change and enjoy being part of it. It is worthwhile looking at one man's contribution to the changing music scene.

Ian Green's involvement with our native music goes back a long way. With roots in the north country, home life meant music in the house when his father's chanter was added to the fiddles and 'moothies' of neighbours and friends. But his origins in the pro-motion of the native music of our land are best traced back some 40 years when as a young police officer he was one of the founders of the Edinburgh Police Folk Club. The folk revival, he recalls, was just starting at the time and the BBC's television programme, Hootenany, brought back happy memories of the music he enjoyed before army service had taken him away from his native heath. Looking back, the real value of his early incursion into the folk field was that it got him involved with singers and musicians, booking talent both known and unknown and receiving the comments of colleagues on the wisdom of his selections. In parallel with this activity grew an involvement in the life of 'Sandy Bells', the focus of the folk scene in Edinburgh. With a realisation that the folk scene was in a disjointed state and there was no ready reference point to find out what was happening in Scotland, Ian with two friends started the Sandy Bells Broadsheet. Pretty soon it was to become more than a two page 'What's On' listing who was attending which folk club. With Ian as co-editor it grew to ten pages and included editorial comment, reviews of albums and interview reports with artistes. The ten years he spent on the broadsheet until more glossy publications came on to the market saw him extend his range of contacts and become a recognisable figure at folk events. The need to raise funds to keep the broadsheet alive encouraged him to try his hand at cassette production an activity which gave him particular satisfaction.

Ian's next step was to set up Discount Folk Records. From a start offering albums for sale at folk events, the idea of a mail order business followed. And when this prospered, there came the realisation that here was something that could be developed when he retired from the Force, something that would, as he put it, 'stop him vegetating'. Within a year of discarding his inspector's uniform, Greentrax Recordings had been formed. The first three albums he produced give an indication of the close links he had established with performers and how they were willing to put their trust in him. The performers were fiddler Ian Hardie, The McCalmans and singer-songwriter Ian Macdonald. Ian's early thoughts were that perhaps up to half a dozen albums a year would be a reasonable output. He had not realised the warmth of the relationship he had built up with artistes over the years. Within a short time, not only the up-and-coming figures were approaching him for recordings but the leading established performers were indicating their interest in working with him. Production jumped to an album a month and then doubled again. Greentrax, undoubtedly, was on its way.

From good sized premises in East Lothian and with his two sons now looking after sales and the accounting side of the business, Ian can reflect on the broadening of his field of activity. Initially concentrating very much on folk music, Greentrax now covers the entire Celtic scene of harp, fiddle, ceilidh and folk-rock. The projection of the right kind of image for Scottish music has always commanded his attention. The sugariness of 'Granny's Hieland Hame' is not for him. While recognising the existence of music hall and its manufactured entertainment, it is the genuine music of Scotland he wants to record for the world. And the business today is truly international. While the States are undoubtedly the largest market, albums of Scottish artistes are going out to Australia, New Zealand, Japan, Taiwan, Greece, Italy, Spain, Portugal, France, Germany, Holland, Poland, Belgium, Denmark and Canada. Ian's comments on what other countries are most receptive to are fascinating. Spain has shown a distinct interest in Gaelic music, the Japanese have a soft spot for harp music and few readers will not know how prominent Germany has become as a provider of work for folk groups, bands and individual artists. And within one country, pockets of favour can be found, especially when a new sound is being offered. The marketplace today is open to the adventurous. This is to be welcomed. Without change there is ossification. Though combining pipes with bongo drums and samba rhythms is no doubt causing many old pipers to stir in their graves, and the noise levels attained by some folk rock bands are not universally acceptable, the sameness of the music performed by many fiddle orchestras on the other hand, warrants some reflection. The Scottish, or Celtic, music scene is vibrant. We must hope that what is good will last; the important thing is to ensure Scottish music will remain definable and recognisable.

Ian Green showing off some of the stars of the folk scene on his Greentrax label

That the number of albums available to the buying public in stores throughout the country has increased dramatically over the years is due in no small measure to the work of Greentrax. Ian though is not slow to comment on the contribution of others. He singles out Jimmy Macgregor for special mention. In the years of the widely listened to *Macgregors Gathering*, Jimmy deftly amalgamated Celtic music with interviews with unusual and interesting characters. Ian welcomes the way today's musicians are willing to cross borders in their playing and cites Robbie Shepherd's Sunday morning programme on Radio Scotland, *The Reel Blend*, as an example of how Scottish music from different genres can be played in turn with acceptance.

The walls of Ian Green's office give an indication of his success in the album production of Scottish music. An East Lothian Business Award hangs beside gold discs awarded by the Scottish Music Industry. One gets the impression he is particularly pleased to have obtained the joint BBC Scotland-Living Tradition 'Album of the Year' Award in 1994, for his Shooglenifty *Venus in Tweeds* album. Special projects which have obviously given him pleasure include the compilation of working songs by various artistes such as Runrig, Christy Moore, Dick Gaughan and The Dubliners celebrate the STUC's 100 of activity. A landmark for all interested in the Scottish music scene was of course the collection of new tunes by contemporary composers bearing the titles *The Nineties Collection* and *The Nineties Collection Volume 2*. These new albums, sponsored by United Distillers and released in association with the Traditional Music and Song Association, feature leading musicians from the various strands that make up the Scottish scene. They are albums which show the tremendous strength and vigour of our native culture. Amongst overseas artistes, one is delighted to see the name of Natalie MacMaster on the Greentrax label.

There is no sign of let-up in the drive that has seen Greentrax develop into such a prominent position in the Scottish music field. In 1997 alone, the company has been active in promoting Scottish music and artistes in France, Canada and Hong Kong, Australia and India.

CHAPTER 19

Pete Heywood and 'The Living Tradition'

THE LIVING TRADITION is the folk world's own magazine. Every two months it pops through the letterbox. Glossy covered, its cargo of features and articles, reports and reviews keeps us well informed about what is happening in the folk scene around the British Isles and, to an extent, further afield.

That there is an authenticity about its pages is not to be wondered at. Pete Heywood, the man at the helm of the magazine, has a full share of music in his blood. As a player, he is happy with a guitar or concertina on his knee, but his natural talents as an organiser flowered early. For 20 years he was at the sharp end organising the annual Girvan Traditional Folk Festival. That would be enough musical involvement for most people, but, for ten years Pete also managed to be the driving force which kept the reputation of Kilmarnock Folk Club to the fore. There only being 24 hours in a day, inevitably the time came when a decision had to be made between his job in the computer field and full-time involvement with music, with or without food. Music won and taking his courage in both hands, the magazine *Living Tradition* was born. It should be said, Pete had the support of his wife. Heather is a very considerable figure at folk festivals and we shall return to her later. What we can say here is that within five years, *Living Tradition* has achieved world-wide sales and is becoming an institution. Orders come in from Alaska to Japan to South Africa and of course all over North and South America. The interest in music which emanates from the British Isles is considerable, and although obviously 'expats' and emigrant stock form the overseas customer nucleus, it should not be thought interest is confined to them. Celtic music in particular continues to make its mark in many places.

Living Tradition is not of course the first attempt to educate and entertain in the folk field using the printed word. *Sandy Bell's Broadsheet* and the *Scottish Folk Gazette* had been given lives because of the sheer dedication of certain individuals. But Pete had a wider vision, and his experience with the Girvan Festival had given him an appreciation of the need for a full-blooded presentation and promotion that would have the strength to reach a wider readership, a readership that would include the casual enthusiast for folk music as well as the out-and-out activist. And he did not intend distribution should halt at the Scottish Border. This has worked to the benefit of Scottish artistes. It has helped them to become known much more quickly outwith their own country, boosted the sales of their albums and encouraged more visitors to travel north to festivals. And it is of course the totality of Scottish music that is being promoted, not just pipe bands, fiddle orchestras and the big names in the folk field. The smaller groups have much to gain.

Living Tradition makes much use of photographs. The magazine's photograph archive, forever growing, contains much of historical value and interest. We will not be unkind and comment about the yesteryear hairstyles and dress of certain performers still prominent today (although the temptation to comment on the hairstyle of one Pete Heywood is considerable). But the magazine does offer a service for those with an interest in such photographs.

With albums being such a major item of importance, both to the recording artistes and the buying public, the magazine gives

Heather Heywood

releases very full coverage. Whether they like it or not, the staff of *Living Tradition* may have to listen to up to 50 albums a month submitted for their opinion. Pete is reluctant to commit himself as to which are his favourite CDs and artistes without a great deal of thought. Put under a little pressure he admits his affection for Heather's *By Yon Castle Wall* which includes her beautiful rendering of 'Paul's Song'. He is quick to make the point it is for others to comment on the significance of that album which owes much to the backing music arranged by Brian McNeill. Pete shows a great respect for the groups that have opened up the folk field. The Clutha he frequently mentions for their pioneer work in breaking new ground with traditional song. He recalls too that that group had two fiddles at a time when fiddle players were not that thick on the ground. His enthusiasm for Aly Bain is unrestricted. He expresses concern that singers may be suffering from a shortage of venues and that small rooms in pubs at present being converted to large open plan spaces may be good for instrumental sessions but not for song get-togethers. There is no doubt that when listening to a singer Pete is also concentrating on the sounds around the voice, be it on a track or in public. On the broader front, he thinks education has a stronger role to play, both in inculcating native culture at an early age and encouraging young people to develop the ability to make their own entertainment.

CHAPTER 20

The Poetry and Prose of Fiddle and Folk

ONE OF THE EARLIEST MUSIC quotes traced is given here to remind readers that tastes in music have always varied, and that evolution is always with us. This quote is attributed to Anacreon, born around 500 BC:

Let them censure, what care I?
The herd of critics I defy.
No, no, the fair, the gay, the young,
Govern the numbers of my song:
All that they approve is sweet,
And all is sense that they repeat.

Allan Ramsay took his music seriously as his *Scots Songs* (spoken to Mrs. N.) shows:

A poem wrote without a thought
By notes may to a song be brought,
Tho' wit be scarce, low the design,
And numbers lame in every line:
But when fair Christy this shall sing
In consort with the trembling string,
Other the poet's often prais'd,
For charms so sweet a voice hath raised.

And a few lines from his 'Ode to the Musick Club' are worth recording:

Each ravisht ear extolls your heavenly art,
Which soothes our care, and elevates the heart,
Whilst hoarser sounds the martial Ardunes move,
And liquid notes invite to shades and love.
Hail safe restorer of distemper'd minds,
That with delight the raging passion binds:
Extatick concord only banisht Hell,
Most perfect when the perfect beings dwell.
Long may our youth attend thy charming rites
Long may they relish thy transporting sweets.

Ramsay, we know, had a sympathetic ear for the pipes:

> *Nor should the martial pibrough be despised,*
> *Own'd and refined by you, these shall the more be prized.*

We cannot say the same for John Couper of Oxford who, writing in *Fables and Tales* in 1720, really put his head on the block:

> *Scotch moggy may go down at Aberdeen,*
> *Where bonnets, bagpipes, and plaids be seen:*
> *But such poor gear no harmony can sute*
> *Much fitter for a Jew's trump than a lute.*

After Ramsay, another son of Edinburgh, Robert Fergusson, would make sure that music would figure in the poetry of our land. But there was a pessimistic streak in Fergusson as his 'Elegy on the Death of Scots Music' would show. He feared continental music would swamp the home product:

> *On Scotia's plains, in days of yore,*
> *When lads and lasses tartan wore,*
> *Saft music rang on ilka shore,*
> *In hamely weid:*
> *But harmony is now no more,*
> *And music dead.*
>
> *At glomin' now the bagpipe's dumb,*
> *Whan weary owsen hameward come;*
> *Sae sweetly as it wont to bum,*
> *And pibrachs skreed;*
> *We never hear its warlike hum;*
> *For music's dead.*
>
> *Macgibbon's gane: Ah! waes my heart!*
> *The man in music maist expert,*
> *Wha cou'd sweet melody impart,*
> *And tune the reed,*
> *Wi' sic a slee and pawky art:*
> *But now he's dead.*
>
> *Now foreign sonnets bear the gree,*
> *And crabbit queer variety*
> *Of sound fresh sprung frae Italy,*
> *A bastard breed!*
> *Unlike that saft-tongu'd melody*

Which now lies dead.
O Scotland! that cou'd yence afford
To bang the pith of Roman sword,
Winna your sons, wi' joint accord,
To battle speed?
And fight till Music be restor'd,
Which now lies dead.

To be fair to Fergusson, he did recognise in 'Auld Reekie' song was
still to be had in the local hostelry:

Now mony a club, jocose and free,
Gie a' to merriment and glee;
Wi' sang and glass, the fley the pow'r
O' care that wad harass the hour.

As if to prove he was the most charismatic figure ever to feature
in musical circles, the most readily available quotes concern Niel
Gow. Many were the lamentations when he died in 1807, the Rev.
James Grahame leading the way:

The blythe strathspey springs up, reminding some
Of nights when Gow's old arm (nor old the tale),
Unceasing, save when reeking cans went round
Made heart and heel leap light as bounding roe.
Alas! No more shall we behold that look
So venerable, yet so blent with mirth,
And festive joy sedate; that ancient garb,
Unvaried; tartan hose and bonnet blue!

Dean Ramsay in his *Reminiscences of Scottish Life and Character*
provides the following:

'Niel was rather addicted to the whisky bottle. On walking
home to Dunkeld, one night, from Perth, where he had been
engaged, as usual, to play the violin at some ball, upon being
asked next day, how he had got home, for it was a long walk, and
he was very tipsy, replied, "that he didna mind the length o' the
road; it was the breadth o' it he cast oot wi'!"'

Dean Ramsay also turned his attention to Scots songs:

'A family belonging to the Scottish Border, after spending
some time at Florence, had returned home, and proud of the
progress they had made in music, the young ladies were anxious

to shew off their accomplishments before an old confidential servant of the family, and accordingly sung to her some of their finest Italian songs which they had learned abroad. Instead, however, of paying them a compliment on their performance, she shewed what she thought of it by asking with much naivete, "Eh, mem, do they ca' skirling like yon singing in foreign parts?"'

Burns made many references to the fiddle in his poems, for example in 'The Jolly Beggars' we have:

> *I am a fiddler to my trade,*
> *An' a' the tunes that e'er I played,*
> *The sweetest still to wife or maid*
> *Was – Whistle owre the lave o't.*

In his Epistle to Major Logan, though, he suggests an intimacy with the instrument:

> *Hale be your heart! Hale be your fiddle!*
> *Lang may your elbuck jink and diddle,*
> *... Come wealth, come poortith, late or soon,*
> *Heaven send your heart-strings ay in tune,*
> *And screw your temper-pins aboon –*
> *A fifth or mair –*
> *The melancholious, lazy croon*
> *O' cankrie care!*

The meeting of Burns with the great Niel Gow has been well reported. But it was William Marshall that Burns declared to be 'the first composer of strathspeys of the age', using Marshall's 'Miss Admiral Gordon's Strathspey' for his 'Of a' the airts the wind can blaw'.

Marshall had four collections of his tunes published. Showing a little irritation at the way some of his tunes were being purloined or maltreated he considered it appropriate to include a note in his 1822 publication that he thought it necessary :

'to mention that several of his strathspeys and reels have occasionally been published by most of the collectors of Scottish music without his permission; of this, however, he does not complain, especially as he had not till now any intention to publish them himself. His only complaint is their not mentioning his name along with those reels of his composition they published, ... in particular, their changing the original names given by him, to other names according to their own fancy.'

James Hogg, 'the Ettrick Shepherd', was a keen fiddler. R.P Gillies describes Hogg's effect on Edinburgh society after a little fame had come his way:

'...cast utterly into the shade by an illiterate shepherd, a man also who seemed to give himself no thought or care about his own works, but to be engaged day after day, or rather night after night, in scraping on the fiddle, singing his own ballads, and, with the help of Glenlivet, making himself and others uproariously happy.'

When it came to song Sir Walter Scott displayed more enthusiasm than singing ability. But Lockhart in his biography of the great man records a fiddle tale of interest. Scott, who was of course a lawyer, had been engaged in a case involving the value of a fiddle and accordingly had had to make himself aware of the famous violin-makers of his day. Then:

'Not long after this, dining at ——, he found himself left alone after dinner with the Duke, who had but two subjects he could talk upon – hunting and music. Having exhausted hunting, Scott thought he would bring forward his lately acquired learning in fiddles, upon which His Grace became quite animated, and immediately whispered some orders to the butler, in consequence of which there soon entered into the room about half a dozen tall footmen, each bearing a fiddle-case; and Scott now found his musical knowledge brought to no less trying a test than of telling, by the tone of each fiddle, as the Duke played it, by what artist it had been made. "By guessing and management", he said, "I got on fairly well, till we were, to my great relief, summoned to coffee."'

Some snippets from around this time:

Play me up Sweet Marie", I cried,
An' loud the piper blew;
But the fiddler played aye Struntum strum,
An' down his bow he threw:
"Now here's thy health i' the red, red wine,
Fair dame o' the stranger land
For never a pair of een before
Could mar my gude bow-hand'.

The Lord's Marie - Allan Cunningham (1784-1842)

'Amongst the rest was a piper, who, for fear of spoiling the delicacy of the touch of his fingers, declined any work unconnected with whisky.'

Memoirs of a Highland Lady – Elizabeth Grant of Rothiemurchus (1797-1830)

Gae bring my guid auld harp ance mair,-
Gae bring it free and fast,-
For I maun sing anither sang,
Ere a' my glee be past.

Scotland Yet – Henry Scott Riddell (1798-1870)

'For many a year, one Robin Boss had been town drummer, with no manner of conduct, saving a very earnest endevour to fill himself fou as often as he could get the means; the consequence of which was, that his face was as plooky as a curran' bun, and his nose as red as a partan's tae.'

The Provost – John Galt

Scott Skinner tried his hand at poetry with 'The Deil's Concert':

My fiddle I strung; an' their chords as they rung,
Set their black blistered shanks a' stirrin'
But, oh, what a yell resounded through Hell
When I struck up the "Miller o' Hirn!

Auld clootie noo arose fae his deep drunken dose,
An' rubbin his bleared een he swore;
'Ye're a gie clever chiel, never man nor yet deil
Play't the fiddle sae finely afore.

Fat treatment ye'll hae I canna just say,
For the fiddlers sent here are but few,
But there's aye place in Hell where there bubbles a well,
And I'll keep that cool corner for you.

Don't forget the one gentleman who had an answer for everything:
... And good pipers iss difficult nooadays to get; there's not many in it. You'll maybe can get a kind of a plain piper going aboot the streets of Gleska noo and then, but they're like the herrin', and the turnips, and rhubarb, and things like that – you don't get them fresh in Gleska; if you want them at their best, you have to go up to the right Hielands and pull them off the tree.'

Para Handy Tales – Neil Munro (Hugh Foulis)

Somehow, we don't associate Prime Ministers with our folk songs and it has to be said not everyone shared his view:

'Dear Mrs Kennedy-Fraser,

Your rescuing from death the songs which belong to the very essence of our being, has indeed revived our own life, and we are happier and stronger and more hopeful – because you have done this for us. We need bread, but we also need song; and of that you have been a most bountiful provider.'

– J. Ramsay MacDonald

To return to strings:

My fiddle's old and so am I.
For it I've often longed in vain.
Bleak years and years I've laid it bye,
But now I'll take it up again.
For in four frail gut strings I know
All music sleeps for me to wake,
And here before the peat-fire glow
Fine melody I'll make.

'Fiddler' – Robert Service

'In particular, the use of the guitar as an accompanying instrument, so far as being a modern nonsense, is a return to a custom which was common enough in earlier days.'

Scotland's Music – Cedric Thorpe Davie

Finally, from an address by Professor Alexander Fenton at the 1994 Folk Art Award to Shetland Fiddlers' Society:

'No musical tradition can afford to be static, because times change, people change, fashions and needs change, and there is a constant influence from the media which has a world wide nature. Where a local tradition has real inner strength, it is well capable of taking on board and adapting all such influences and making them again something uniquely local, even though in some degree different from the tradition of fifty or a hundred years before.'

Acknowledgements

My first expression of thanks must go to those individual artistes and groups whose life stories, anecdotes and opinions make up the body of this book. Every single person I approached was willing to sit down with me and discuss their involvement in the Scottish, and often wider, music scene. They did this with complete frankness, and, I must add, courteously accepted the more personal questions put to them. It has been a refreshing exercise for me, and speaks volumes for our artistes, who, while at home on the international stage, also consistently reminded me we are all part of a family headed by a Mr and Mrs Jock Tamson. Music is indeed a wonderful catalyst for friendship.

For providing me with a general music overview and clarification on governmental interest in the promotion of our Scottish culture and heritage I have been fortunate to have had ready access to Dave Francis, Director of the Edinburgh Folk Festival, who is currently carrying out a project on behalf of the Scottish Arts Council. Dave's wealth of experience in the traditional and folk field from band leader to administrator was willingly placed at my disposal.

Further north, Mary Milne of Banchory with her anecdotes and Scott Skinner artefacts reminded me of how much enjoyment, perhaps fulfilment is a better word, the fiddle has given to thousands and thousands of Scots over times good and bad. Because of the scant mention they receive in the text, I express my thanks here to James Calder for providing me with information about the Edinburgh Highland Strathspey and Reel Society, Charlotte Findlater for her advice about the Glasgow Caledonian Strathspey and Reel Society and Anna Simpson for sharing with me her enthusiasm for the Shetland Fiddlers' Society. And I have to say that even where the involvement in the Scottish music scene has been essentially of a commercial nature, the enthusiasm of those spoken to left me in no doubt that maintaining the integrity of our native culture was ahead of purely business considerations.

To publishers Methuen & Co. Ltd. I am grateful for permission to quote from *The Ballad Tree* by Evelyn Kendrick Wells.

For giving me permission to reproduce their photographs I would particularly thank:

Mairi Campbell (p106)
Alistair Chafer – Living Tradition (pp4, 7, 129)
Peter Fairbairn – Living Tradition (pp15, 17, 45)
Hamish Henderson (pp20, 22)
Brian McNeill (p29)

Eddie McGuire (p36)
John Mason (p49)
Gordon Hotchkiss (pp54, 66)
Dougie MacLean (p56)
Hamish Moore/Marc Marnie, Stagefright Productions (p61)
The National Trust for Scotland (p71)
Mary Milne (p81)
Elisabeth McLay (p83)
Anna Simpson (p87)
Jim Reid (p93)
Ian Green (pp97, 126)
Fiona Ritchie (p111)

Finally, with affection, I declare my debt to my wife Helen. For months now she has willingly forsaken her own music-making and composing activities to read, query, check and edit drafts and listen to recordings. Bravely she has kept her own opinions at bay and while making allowance for my idiosyncrasies, has generally kept me pointed in the right direction. The safe arrival of this book on the shelves owes much to her.

Some other books published by **LUATH** PRESS

MUSIC AND DANCE

Highland Balls and Village Halls

GW Lockhart
ISBN 0 946487 12 X   PBK   £6.95

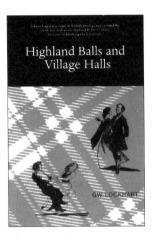

Acknowledged as a classic in Scottish dancing circles throughout the world. Anecdotes, Scottish history, dress and dance steps are all included in this

'*delightful little book, full of interest…
both a personal account and an understanding look at the making of traditions.*'
NEW ZEALAND SCOTTISH COUNTRY DANCES MAGAZINE

'*A delightful survey of Scottish dancing and custom. Informative, concise and opinionated, it guides the reader across the history and geography of country dance and ends by detailing the 12 dances every Scot should know – the most famous being the Eightsome Reel, "the greatest longest, rowdiest, most diabolically executed of all the Scottish country dances".*'
THE HERALD

'*A pot-pourri of every facet of Scottish country dancing. It will bring back memories of petronella turns and poussettes and make*

you eager to take part in a Broun's reel or a dashing white sergeant!'
DUNDEE COURIER AND ADVERTISER

'*An excellent an very readable insight into the traditions and customs of Scottish country dancing. The author takes us on a tour from his own early days jigging in the village hall to the characters and traditions that have made our own brand of dance popular throughout the world.*'
SUNDAY POST

BIOGRAPHY

On the Trail of Robert Service

GW Lockhart
ISBN 0 946487 24 3   PBK   £7.95
Known worldwide for his verses 'The Shooting of Dan McGrew' and 'The Cremation of Sam McGee', Service has woven his spell for Boy Scouts and learned professors alike. He chronicled the story of the Klondike Gold Rush, wandered the United States and Canada, Tahiti and Russia to become the bigger-than-life Bard of the Yukon. Whether you love or hate him, you can't ignore this cult figure. The book is a must for those who haven't yet met Robert Service.

'*The story of a man who claimed that he wrote verse for those who wouldn't be seen dead reading poetry… this enthralling biography will delight Service lovers in both the Old World and the New.*'
SCOTS INDEPENDENT

Bare Feet and Tackety Boots

Archie Cameron
ISBN 0 946487 17 0   PBK   £7.95
The island of Rum before the First World War was the playground of its rich absentee landowner. A survivor of life a century gone tells his story. Factors and schoolmasters, midges and poaching, deer, ducks and MacBrayne's steamers: here social history and personal anecdote create a record of a way of life gone not long ago but already almost forgotten. This is the story the gentry couldn't tell.

'This book is an important piece of social history, for it gives an insight into how the other half lived in an era the likes of which will never be seen again'
FORTHRIGHT MAGAZINE

'The authentic breath of the pawky, country-wise estate employee.'
THE OBSERVER

'Well observed and detailed account of island life in the early years of this century'
THE SCOTS MAGAZINE

'A very good read with the capacity to make the reader chuckle. A very talented writer.'
STORNOWAY GAZETTE

Come Dungeons Dark

John Taylor Caldwell
ISBN 0 946487 19 7 PBK £6.95
Glasgow anarchist Guy Aldred died with 10p in his pocket in 1963 claiming there was better company in Barlinnie Prison than in the Corridors of Power. 'The Red Scourge' is remembered here by one who worked with him and spent 27 years as part of his turbulent household, sparring with Lenin, Sylvia Pankhurst and others as he struggled for freedom for his beloved fellow-man.

'The welcome and long-awaited biography of... one of this country's most prolific radical propagandists... Crank or visionary?... whatever the verdict, the Glasgow anarchist has finally been given a fitting memorial.'
THE SCOTSMAN

POETRY

Blind Harry's Wallace

William Hamilton of Gilbertfield
ISBN 0 946487 43 X HBK £15.00
ISBN 0 946487 33 2 PBK £7.50
The original story of the real braveheart, Sir William Wallace. Racy, blood on every page, violently anglophobic, grossly embellished, vulgar and disgusting, clumsy and stilted, a literary failure, a great epic. Whatever the verdict on BLIND HARRY, this is the book which has done more than any other to frame the notion of Scotland's national identity. Despite its numerous 'historical inaccuracies', it remains the principal source for what we now know about the life of Wallace.

The novel and film *Braveheart* were based on the 1722 Hamilton edition of this epic poem. Burns, Wordsworth, Byron and others were greatly influenced by this version 'wherein the old obsolete words are rendered more intelligible', which is said to be the book, next to the Bible, most commonly found in Scottish households in the eighteenth century. Burns even admits to having 'borrowed... a couplet worthy of Homer' directly from Hamilton's version of BLIND HARRY to include in 'Scots wha hae'.

Elspeth King, in her introduction to this, the first accessible edition of BLIND HARRY in verse form since 1859, draws parallels between the situation in Scotland at the time of Wallace and that in Bosnia and Chechnya in the 1990s. Seven hundred years to the day after the Battle of Stirling Bridge, the 'Settled Will of the Scottish People' was expressed in the devolution referendum of 11 September 1997. She describes this as a landmark opportunity for mature reflection on how the nation has been shaped, and sees BLIND HARRY'S WALLACE as an essential and compelling text for this purpose.

'Builder of the literary foundations of a national hero-cult in a free and powerful country'.
ALEXANDER STODDART, sculptor

'A true bard of the people'
TOM SCOTT, THE PENGUIN BOOK OF
SCOTTISH VERSE, on Blind Harry.

'A more inventive writer than Shakespeare'
RANDALL WALLACE

'The story of Wallace poured a Scottish prejudice in my veins which will boil along until the floodgates of life shut in eternal rest'
ROBERT BURNS

'Hamilton's couplets are not the best poetry you will ever read, but they rattle along at a fair pace. In re-issuing this work, the publishers have re-opened the spring from which most of our conceptions of the Wallace legend come'.
SCOTLAND ON SUNDAY

'The return of Blind Harry's Wallace, a man who makes Mel look like a wimp'.
THE SCOTSMAN

The Jolly Beggars or 'Love and Liberty'

Robert Burns
ISBN 0 946487 02 2 HB £8.00
Forgotten by the Bard himself, the rediscovery of this manuscript caused storms of acclaim at the turn of the 19th century. Yet it is hardly known today. It was set to music to form the only cantata ever written by Burns. SIR WALTER SCOTT wrote: 'Laid in the very lowest department of low life, the actors being a set of strolling vagrants... extravagant glee and outrageous frolic... not, perhaps, to be paralleled in the English language.' This edition is printed in Burns' own handwriting with an informative introduction by Tom Atkinson.

'The combination of facsimile, lively John Hampson graphics and provocative comment on the text makes for enjoyable reading.'
THE SCOTSMAN

Poems to be Read Aloud

selected and introduced by Tom Atkinson
ISBN 0 946487 00 6 PBK £5.00
This personal collection of doggerel and verse ranging from the tear-jerking 'Green Eye of the Yellow God' to the rarely-printed bawdy 'Eskimo Nell' has a lively cult following. Much borrowed and rarely returned, this is a book for reading aloud in very good company, preferably after a dram or twa. You are guaranteed a warm welcome if you arrive at a gathering with this little volume in your pocket.

'The essence is the audience.'
Tom Atkinson

FOLKLORE

The Supernatural Highlands

Francis Thompson
ISBN 0 946487 31 6 PBK £8.99
An authoritative exploration of the otherworld of the Highlander, happenings and beings hitherto thought to be outwith the ordinary forces of nature. A simple introduction to the way of life of rural Highland and Island communities, this new edition weaves a path through second sight, the evil eye, witchcraft, ghosts, fairies and other supernatural beings, offering new sight-lines on areas of belief once dismissed as folklore and superstition.

LUATH GUIDES TO SCOTLAND

'Gentlemen, We have just returned from a six week stay in Scotland. I am convinced that Tom Atkinson is the best guidebook author I have ever read, about any place, any time.'
Edward Taylor, LOS ANGELES

These guides are not your traditional where-to-stay and what-to-eat books. They are companions in the rucksack or car seat, providing the discerning traveller with a blend of fiery opinion and moving description. Here you will find 'that curious pastiche of myths and legend and history that the Scots use to describe their heritage... what battle happened in which glen between which clans; where the Picts sacrificed bulls as recently as the

17th century... A lively counterpoint to the more standard, detached guidebook... Intriguing.'
These are perfect guides for the discerning visitor or resident to keep close by for reading again and again, written by authors who invite you to share their intimate knowledge and love of the areas covered.

South West Scotland

Tom Atkinson

ISBN 0 946487 04 9 PBK £4.95

This descriptive guide to the magical country of Robert Burns covers Kyle, Carrick, Galloway, Dumfries-shire, Kirkcudbrightshire and Wigtownshire. Hills, unknown moors and unspoiled beaches grace a land steeped in history and legend and portrayed with affection and deep delight.

An essential book for the visitor who yearns to feel at home in this land of peace and grandeur.

The Lonely Lands

Tom Atkinson

ISBN 0 946487 10 3 PBK £4.95

A guide to Inveraray, Glencoe, Loch Awe, Loch Lomond, Cowal, the Kyles of Bute and all of central Argyll written with insight, sympathy and loving detail. Once Atkinson has taken you there, these lands can never feel lonely. 'I have sought to make the complex simple, the beautiful accessible and the strange familiar,' he writes, and indeed he brings to the land a knowledge and affection only accessible to someone with intimate knowledge of the area.

A must for travellers and natives who want to delve beneath the surface.

'Highly personal and somewhat quirky... steeped in the lore of Scotland.'

The Empty Lands

Tom Atkinson

ISBN 0 946487 13 8 PBK £4.95

The Highlands of Scotland from Ullapool to Bettyhill and Bonar Bridge to John O'Groats are landscapes of myth and legend, 'empty of people, but of nothing else that brings delight to any tired soul,' writes Atkinson. This highly personal guide describes Highland history and landscape with love, compassion and above all sheer magic.

Essential reading for anyone who has dreamed of the Highlands.

Roads to the Isles

Tom Atkinson

ISBN 0 946487 01 4 PBK £4.95

Ardnamurchan, Morvern, Morar, Moidart and the west coast to Ullapool are included in this guide to the Far West and Far North of Scotland. An unspoiled land of mountains, lochs and silver sands is brought to the walker's toe-tips (and to the reader's fingertips) in this stark, serene and evocative account of town, country and legend. For any visitor to this Highland wonderland, Queen Victoria's favourite place on earth.

Highways and Byways in Mull and Iona

Peter Macnab

ISBN 0 946487 16 2 PBK £4.25

'The Isle of Mull is of Isles the fairest,
Of ocean's gems 'tis the first and rarest.'
So a local poet described it a hundred years ago, and this recently revised guide to Mull and sacred Iona, the most accessible islands of the Inner Hebrides, takes the reader on a delightful tour of these rare ocean gems, travelling with a native whose unparalleled knowledge and deep feeling for the area unlock the byways of the islands in all their natural beauty.

NATURAL SCOTLAND

Rum: Nature's Island

Magnus Magnusson KBE

ISBN 0 946487 32 4   £7.95 PBK

Rum: Nature's Island is the fascinating story of a Hebridean island from the earliest times through to the Clearances and its period as the sporting playground of a Lancashire industrial magnate, and on to its rebirth as a National Nature Reserve, a model for the active ecological management of Scotland's wild places.

Thoroughly researched and written in a lively accessible style, the book includes comprehensive coverage of the island's geology, animals and plants, and people, with a special chapter on the Edwardian extravaganza of Kinloch Castle. There is practical information for visitors to what was once known as 'the Forbidden Isle'; the book provides details of bothy and other accommodation, walks and nature trails. It closes with a positive vision for the island's future: biologically diverse, economically dynamic and ecologically sustainable.

Rum: Nature's Island is published in co-operation with Scottish Natural Heritage (of which Magnus Magnusson is Chairman) to mark the 40th anniversary of the acquisition of Rum by its predecessor, The Nature Conservancy.

WALK WITH LUATH

Mountain Days & Bothy Nights

Dave Brown and Ian Mitchell

ISBN 0 946487 15 4   PBK   £7.50

Acknowledged as a classic of mountain writing still in demand ten years after its first publication, this book takes you into the bothies, howffs and dosses on the Scottish hills. Fishgut Mac, Desperate Dan and Stumpy the Big Yin stalk hill and public house, evading gamekeepers and Royalty with a camaraderie which was the trademark of Scots hillwalking in the early days.

'The fun element comes through... how innocent the social polemic seems in our nastier world of today... the book for the rucksack this year.'
Hamish Brown, SCOTTISH MOUNTAINEERING CLUB JOURNAL

'The doings, sayings, incongruities and idiosyncrasies of the denizens of the bothy underworld... described in an easy philosophical style... an authentic word picture of this part of the climbing scene in latter-day Scotland, which, like any good picture, will increase in charm over the years.'
Iain Smart, SCOTTISH MOUNTAINEERING CLUB JOURNAL

'The ideal book for nostalgic hillwalkers of the 60s, even just the armchair and public house variety... humorous, entertaining, informative, written by two men with obvious expertise, knowledge and love of their subject.'
SCOTS INDEPENDENT

'Fifty years have made no difference. Your crowd is the one I used to know... [This] must be the only complete dossers' guide ever put together.'
Alistair Borthwick, author of the immortal *Always a Little Further.*

The Joy of Hillwalking

Ralph Storer

ISBN 0 946487 28 6   PBK   £6.95

Apart, perhaps, from the joy of sex, the joy of hillwalking brings more pleasure to more people than any other form of human activity.

'Alps, America, Scandinavia, you name it – Storer's been there, so why the hell shouldn't he bring all these various and varied places into his observations... [He] even admits to losing his virginity after a day on the Aggy Ridge... Well worth its place alongside Storer's earlier works.'
TAC

LUATH WALKING GUIDES

The highly respected and continually updated guides to the Cairngorms.

'Particularly good on local wildlife and how to see it'
THE COUNTRYMAN

Walks in the Cairngorms

Ernest Cross
ISBN 0 946487 09 X PBK £3.95

This selection of walks celebrates the rare birds, animals, plants and geological wonders of a region often believed difficult to penetrate on foot. Nothing is difficult with this guide in your pocket, as Cross gives a choice for every walker, and includes valuable tips on mountain safety and weather advice.

Ideal for walkers of all ages and skiers waiting for snowier skies.

Short Walks in the Cairngorms

Ernest Cross
ISBN 0 946487 23 5 PBK £3.95

Cross wrote this volume after overhearing a walker remark that there were no short walks for lazy ramblers in the Cairngorm region. Here is the answer: rambles through scenic woods with a welcoming pub at the end, birdwatching hints, glacier holes, or for the fit and ambitious, scrambles up hills to admire vistas of glorious scenery. Wildlife in the Cairngorms is unequalled elsewhere in Britain, and here it is brought to the binoculars of any walker who treads quietly and with respect.

SOCIAL HISTORY

The Crofting Years

Francis Thompson
ISBN 0 946487 06 5 PBK £6.95

Crofting is much more than a way of life. It is a storehouse of cultural, linguistic and moral values which holds together a scattered and struggling rural population. This book fills a blank in the written history of crofting over the last two centuries. Bloody conflicts and gunboat diplomacy, treachery, compassion, music and story: all figure in this mine of information on crofting in the Highlands and Islands of Scotland.

'I would recommend this book to all who are interested in the past, but even more so to those who are interested in the future survival of our way of life and culture'
STORNOWAY GAZETTE

'A cleverly planned book... the story told in simple words which compel attention... [by] a Gaelic speaking Lewisman with specialised knowledge of the crofting community.'
BOOKS IN SCOTLAND

'The book is a mine of information on many aspects of the past, among them the homes, the food, the music and the medicine of our crofting forebears.'
John M Macmillan, erstwhile CROFTERS COMMISSIONER FOR LEWIS AND HARRIS

'This fascinating book is recommended to anyone who has the interests of our language and culture at heart.'
Donnie Maclean, DIRECTOR OF AN COMUNN GAIDHEALACH, WESTERN ISLES

'Unlike many books on the subject, Crofting Years combines a radical political approach to Scottish crofting experience with a ruthless realism which while recognising the full tragedy and difficulty of his subject never descends to sentimentality or nostalgia'
CHAPMAN

Luath Press Limited

committed to publishing well written books worth reading

LUATH PRESS takes its name from Robert Burns, whose little collie
Luath (*Gael.*, swift or nimble) tripped up Jean Armour at a wedding and
gave him the chance to speak to the woman who was to be his wife and the
abiding love of his life. Burns called one of *The Twa Dogs* Luath after
Cuchullin's hunting dog in Ossian's Fingal. Luath Press grew up in the
heart of Burns country, and now resides a few steps up the road from Burns'
first lodgings in Edinburgh's Royal Mile.
Luath offers you distinctive writing with a hint of unexpected pleasures.

Most UK bookshops either carry our books in stock or can order them for
you. To order direct from us, please send a £sterling cheque, postal order,
international money order or your credit card details (number, address of
cardholder and expiry date) to us at the address below. Please add post and
packing as follows: UK – £1.00 per delivery address; overseas surface mail
– £2.50 per delivery address; overseas airmail – £3.50 for the first book to
each delivery address, plus £1.00 for each additional book by airmail to the
same address. If your order is a gift, we will happily enclose your card or
message at no extra charge.

Luath Press Limited
543/2 Castlehill
The Royal Mile
Edinburgh EH1 2ND

Telephone: 0131 225 4326
Fax: 0131 225 4324
email: gavin.macdougall@luath.co.uk
Website: www.luath.co.uk